shops & boutiques 2000

designer stores and brand imagery

shops&boutiques
&2000
designer stores and brand imagery

PBC International Incorporated

Susan Abramson   Marcie Stuchin

foreword by
kate spade
NEW YORK

Distributor to the book trade in the United States and Canada
Rizzoli International Publications Inc., through St. Martin's Press
175 Fifth Avenue, New York, NY 10010

All other distribution
PBC International Incorporated
One School Street
Glen Cove, New York 11542

For a free catalog
PBC International Incorporated
One School Street, Glen Cove, New York 11542
1-800-527-2826, within New York State 516-676-2727
e-mail: PBCINTL@AOL.COM

Library of Congress Cataloging-in-Publication Data available

ISBN 0-86636-687-3

CAVEAT—Information in this text is believed accurate, and will
pose no problem for the student or casual reader. However, the
author was often constrained by information contained in signed
release forms, information that could have been in error or not
included at all. Any misinformation (or lack of information) is the
result of failure in these attestations. The author has done what-
ever is possible to insure accuracy.

10 9 8 7 6 5 4 3 2 1   Printed in Hong Kong

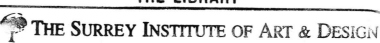

In memory of Bernie Ozer, mentor and friend.
His passion and originality continues to inspire
the world of fashion and merchandising.

s.a.

For Mark,
Whose style, taste and creativity are second to none!

m.s.

foreword

Today more than ever, the purpose a store serves is being challenged. Previously seen almost exclusively as a profit center, stores are now being used to achieve this objective and much more. Increasingly, they are looked at as advertising vehicles, laboratories for product line experimentation, resources providing important information about the customer, and a means to position brands adjacent to their competitors, both in terms of location and in the minds of the customer.

Depending on the goals of the company, a store can serve any number of these purposes. The overarching purpose of most major brand retail environments is to communicate the company's sensibility, achieving a secure and well-defined position with their target customer. How this purpose is balanced with other objectives can be achieved in a variety of ways. While a simplification of retail strategy, I've recognized three primary approaches.

The first approach could be defined as the Monument to the Brand. Most often this involves a very clear vision which drives the company's marketing strategy. A designer or company leader, working closely with an architect of stature, defines a large-scale store environment down to the smallest detail. From the architecture and packaging to the sales staff and music, these stores communicate the company's vision in its purest articulation. They are often loss leaders, giving up in profit what they gain in brand awareness and connection with the customer. Strategically placed in major cities around the world, these stores serve to enhance the brand image via high foot traffic, PR, and competitive brand adjacencies. This approach is, at its core, a very American approach to marketing.

Another approach to the store environment is the classic boutique. A more European approach, the boutique exudes coziness and a personal touch that sends the message "We're here to sell beautiful merchandise, not architecture." A more human scale creates an environment which is both welcoming and intriguing to the customer. The merchandise mix is often eclectic or very selectively bought and displayed. Rather than communicating through a museum-like setting where items are treated in a precious manner and "Don't touch" is the underlying message, visitors to these boutiques are invited to interact with the merchandise and feel at home. While both models serve an important purpose, the boutique is less marketing driven and yet, if successful, thrives on the loyalty of its customers to its particular smaller scale brand personality.

Finally, there is a combination of the grand scale brand monument and the intimate boutique. These stores communicate, through architecture and atmosphere, the essence of the brand. Most nuances are considered and a level of comfort for the customer is taken into consideration. Ideally, profitability and brand identification are both achieved. Companies large and small may find this approach effective, based on their priorities and sensibility.

In the end, each company has to decide what primary purpose the store is to serve. The successful boutique mirrors the vision of the company's designer or leader. This vision sets the tone for the brand and every element therein—from product to stores, advertising to customer service. The interior design of stores of every shape and size sends a message to the customer and creates an emotional response. Thankfully, it is because there exists such a diversity of creative vision that there is an increasingly fascinating and unique retail landscape.

Kate Spade
Founder & Designer

Andy Spade
Founder, Creative Director & acting CEO

kate spade
NEW YORK

introduction

What's in a name?

In the world of retailing today, it seems like everything.

The major industry forces, including *Ralph Lauren*, *Calvin Klein*, *Giorgio Armani*, *Valentino*, *Chanel*, *Donna Karan*, and *Tommy Hilfiger*, are internationally recognized brands with clear proprietary images. In the highly competitive retail environment of the late 1990s, designer boutiques and branded stores have created a one-world market that speaks a universal language. Consumers select one brand's product over another because of the value added by its perceived image. They buy the labels they know because of the life-styles they represent.

Manufacturers Are Retailers, Too

As brand and image builders strive for individual signatures that distinguish their labels from others, they are redefining the aesthetics of marketing and reinventing store design. Manufacturers, vying for increased exposure and market share, have discovered a new option. They, too, can be retailers. In company owned and licensed freestanding stores, manufacturers are building brand equity and shaping an experience around complete collections. Essentially billboards for their labels, designer stores attain maximum control of the product and its consistent presentation, and become the ultimate personal and professional expressions of their namesake designers.

Flagships and freestanding designer stores do not come cheap. Often considered loss-leaders in high-rent neighborhoods, they are bold, expensive tributes to the designers' aesthetic. The increased exposure is not only an image enhancer, but it also gives brands greater leverage with major department store chains.

As the Year 2000 Approaches, Retail Design Has a New Aesthetic

In recent years, designers and merchants have collaborated with internationally acclaimed architects, interior designers and image makers to develop their own stores. Working together, they have created environments and identity elements that embody the lifestyles millions of customers wish to embrace.

Shops & Boutiques 2000: Designer Stores and Brand Imagery illustrates the most forward trends in international retail design. Many boutiques—like *Calvin Klein* and *Dolce & Gabbana*, New York City, *Emporio Armani*, *Bal Harbour*, *Kate Spade*, Los Angeles, and *DKNY*, Berlin— are spare and modern, allowing their minimalist styles to take center stage. Others—such as *Polo Ralph Lauren*, Phoenix, and the *Chanel Jewellery* boutique in Paris—express classic luxury, much like that of their timeless products. Some—including *MacKenzie-Childs* and *Quiksilver Boardriders Club*, both in New York—are pure fun and fantasy, filled with whimsical displays. Pulsing music and exciting visuals underscore the youthful spirit promoted by *Tommy Hilfiger* and *Guess?* in Beverly Hills, *Diesel* in San Francisco, and *Steve Madden* in SoHo.

The trend-setting stores we chose for this volume express their designers' aesthetic sensibilities through inventive architecture and interior design. All are designed to project an identity or promote a lifestyle. All possess levels of sophistication and creativity that cleverly transform traditional store merchandising into dramatic stage sets, placing the designers' collections on view for the whole world to see. These innovative shops and boutiques are influencing store design today and will determine retail trends in the twenty-first century.

Susan Abramson   **Marcie Stuchin**

master

CLASS

tommy hilfiger

Tommy Hilfiger's merchandising goal is clear: produce a high quality product, enhance the brand name to boost label recognition and continually increase sales. With global name recognition on a par with Coke and MTV, and dozens of company-owned stores in the U.S. and overseas, Tommy Hilfiger is continually boosting its image. The first flagship on Rodeo Drive, Beverly Hills, was designed in the spirit of Hilfiger's muse—American youth. Hilfiger selected "the best of his best" and placed it in 21,000 square feet of casual retail space at the epicenter of the music and entertainment worlds, where pop culture reigns.

Boasting the largest frontage on Rodeo Drive, the flagship's all-white exterior, designed by Washington, D.C.-based architect Allan Greenberg, is a tribute to classic American style. With stately columns and a rotunda, it conjures images of a miniature White House. The interior, designed by Jerry Robertson, continues the all-Americana mood, focusing on a dramatic domed ceiling and a majestic staircase that connects the first floor with the second. Men's merchandise is housed on the first floor; women's and children's are on the second.

Choosing from the myriad styles and licensees of Tommy Hilfiger merchandise—Tommy Jeans, men's and women's clothing, childrenswear, accessories, home collection, fragrance and beauty—the Beverly Hills flagship showcases a carefully edited collection that pays homage to the company's ties to music, entertainment, and fashion. Throughout the store, the Tommy Hilfiger rock 'n roll image pervades. Of particular note is the section that displays a collection of Hilfiger clothing designed for rock stars. Rock-themed art, including photos of performers and Andy Warhol's "Mick Jagger," lines the walls.

As a laboratory for the newest Hilfiger products, the store has introduced a high-end line of men's and women's wear, sold exclusively at the Beverly Hills store. In addition, a new infant's and toddler's collection and a prototype in-store shop for the new line of unisex beauty products were inaugurated here.

Tommy Hilfiger's devotion to detail transcends his familiar red-white-and-blue logo, crested shirts, and urban prep look. Adhering to the prolific designer's belief that dressing rooms should be spacious and comfortable, Hilfiger and Robertson decorated them in styles indicative of the customers using them—for kids, the wallpaper is cheerful gingham, women's don delicate ticking, and men's are dressed in utility denim. Since Hilfiger considers music to be conducive to buying, a sound system that rivals a recording studio projects specially selected mixes that fortify the hip-hop attitude.

architect
ALLAN GREENBERG, ARCHITECT, LLC

interior designer
TOMMY HILFIGER U.S.A., INC.

photographer
CHARLES WHITE

square feet/meters   21,000/1,951

design budget   not disclosed

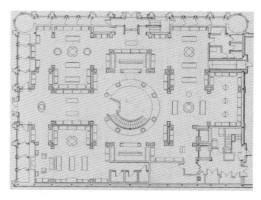

"There is only one Mademoiselle
in the world, and that is I;
one Madame, and that is Rubinstein
and one Miss, and that is Arden."
Coco Chanel, 1936

"First there must be Salons."
Elizabeth Arden, 1920

elizabeth arden

The creation of a brand image emerges, in large part, from aesthetics and style—the look of the product, its packaging and advertising campaign, the design of its stores. Yet brand image, however well-established, doesn't last forever. Companies are compelled to redesign and redefine. The reinvention of Elizabeth Arden's famed Fifth Avenue flagship reveals the possibilities for an all-American classic.

Retaining the signature red door at the entrance and period architectural details of the landmarked Elizabeth Arden building, the design firm of JGA, Inc has completed the renovation of the 1,500-square-foot shop. JGA has created a classically modern retail environment with the ambience of an intimate residential dressing room—much like Miss Arden's might have looked were she alive today. The design, inspired by the gentle arch of the barrel-vaulted ceiling, features softly rounded fixtures of limed oak trimmed with gold tassel hardware. Makeup and treatment products are presented on curved fixtures that line one side of the narrow shop; display units alternate with vanity tables. On the opposite wall, fragrance takes the spotlight in narrow, arcade-like bays. A freestanding color unit, placed front and center, was designed to mimic delicate boudoir furnishings.

The street level Elizabeth Arden boutique is at once a retail venue and a reception area for the full service salon upstairs. Entering through the store, salon clients become immersed in Arden lore and visual merchandising before proceeding to the dramatic elevator bank, also designed by JGA, Inc. Multiple coats of shocking "Red Door Red" lacquer support the brand identity program, enveloping customers in a gallery of Arden heritage.

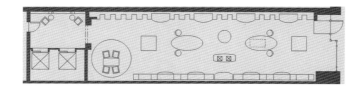

architect
WJCA, INC.

interior designer
JGA, INC

photographer
LASZLO REGOS

square feet/meters   1,500/139

design budget   not disclosed

bvlgari

Bvlgari has epitomized exquisite Italian style and quality in jewelry for more than 100 years. When Bvlgari's in-house architectural team collaborated with New York architect Marco Carrano on the 1997 renovation of the firm's flagship Fifth Avenue store, the team bestowed the same painstaking care on the building's alteration as Bvlgari's designers lavish on its jewelry. They ensured that the design of the new space reflects Bvlgari's dedication to translating classic Italian design into distinctive contemporary expressions.

The current façade of the limestone building, while impressive, no longer appears impenetrable. Windows have been added, allowing shoppers a glimpse into the modern store and providing natural light for the interior. A glass revolving front door has replaced a closed entry and old-fashioned buzzer system. The new first floor gallery is almost twice the size of its predecessor. The designers combined numerous small rooms into one large, open space that allows customers to browse leisurely among the polished wood display islands. A few private viewing rooms are still available on request.

A soft, peach-toned color scheme complements the pearwood cabinetry. Delicate sycamore strips woven with Rosa Asiago and bush-hammered Botticino Italian marble also enhance the interior.

The second floor is dedicated exclusively to fragrances and accessories, including a silk collection, leather goods and eyewear. The Bvlgari café, with its bronze and pearwood bar, entices clients to linger over cappuccino and panini.

Bvlgari employs its in-house architectural team for the design of all of its stores, ensuring a consistent image for the prestigious Italian brand. There are currently three locations in New York City and 60 shops worldwide.

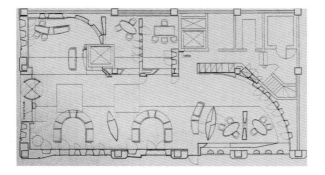

architects/interior designers
BVLGARI
MARCO CARRANO ASSOCIATES

photographer
ANTONIA MULAS

square feet/meters   5,000/465

design budget   not disclosed

bernardaud

With its pristine tile floors, comfortably sleek sofas, and grand ceiling heights, the Bernardaud flagship on New York's Park Avenue looks like a chic Parisian apartment. It is, in fact, a retail showcase for one of the world's finest producers of Limoges porcelain and tabletop accessories. Having come a long way from the days of Napoleon III, when the firm was founded, the Bernardaud of today bridges the gap between old world and new. The store, designed by renowned French designer Olivier Gagnère with a refined, modern sensibility, is a meeting ground for the past, present, and future.

Olivier Gagnère has been associated with Bernardaud since the early 1990s, when he first began designing fine porcelains for the company. Within a short time, the impact of his inventive, decorative designs set the standard for a new style of quirky elegance. His signature Black Tulip group is said to be the porcelain equivalent of Prada's nylon backpack.

Although the Bernardaud line is sold to thousands of retailers throughout the world, nowhere is its presentation so elegant and complete as in the coolly polished, Gagnère-designed New York shop. Appealing to the lifestyles of young, affluent professionals, classic and contemporary styles are displayed together in liveable vignettes arranged in more than 20 vitrines and showcases. Throughout the 3,000-square-foot space, Gagnère's familiar ribbon-stripes appear on table bases and wall sconces. Gagnère's custom upholstered furniture elegantly complements Bernardaud's merchandising program.

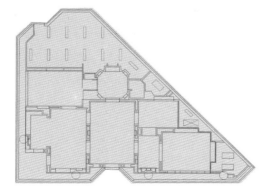

architect/interior designer
BERNARDAUD

photographer
NOEL ALLUM

square feet/meters   3,000/279
design budget $500,000

cole haan

Throughout the world, the name Cole Haan symbolizes fine leather shoes, bags and accessories. Its retail stores, located in major cities across the United States, reflect the company's unwavering attention to detail, quality and materials. While retail environments in separate cities differ somewhat due to regional appeal and size restrictions, all Cole Haan stores promote a timeless signature style. Forbes Shea, the architectural firm based near Cole Haan corporate headquarters in Maine, has designed all the retail locations.

Although the company's timeless image is always paramount in design, Forbes Shea has flavored the Houston installation with a contemporary Texas flair. The building's exterior features a Southwestern-style wood portico over an enormous curved glass window, establishing the feeling of a freestanding flagship for a store attached to a large shopping center.

Two oversized bronze entry doors provide access into Cole Haan. The most exclusive feature of this store is the distinctive bas-relief sculpture of wild palomino ponies executed by Lucille Patino, a local artist. All facets of the Houston store reveal an artistic touch. Custom cabinetry and display tables by Mike Bell of Chicago are made of bleached European hardwoods. Walls and ceilings are covered and highly polished in a lustrous Venetian-style plaster application on a base of powdered marble and chalk.

Cole Haan's New York City store, one of its most important showcases, is located at the heart of prime Madison Avenue real estate. For this 2,500-square-foot site, Forbes Shea has created a new look, now the prototype for other retail outlets. Merchandise is no longer compartmentalized, but presented in mahogany vitrines arranged by lifestyle activity. This allows customers to easily coordinate shoes and accessories.

To open up the deep narrow space, the architects have installed a 30-foot vaulted ceiling. A light fixture, made of onyx with bronze and nickel detailing, hangs dramatically from above. All other fixtures in the store have metal finishes. Merchandise is illuminated by low-voltage halogen track lighting set inside the vitrines. An elliptical cashwrap surfaced with black Andes granite allows for smooth flow of traffic.

Cole Haan's San Francisco storefront on Union Square boasts an impressive new bronze, stone and glass facade. Strong bronze vertical and spandrel pieces are intended to blend with the overall character of the building, which dates to the early 1900s. The interior has also been designed to complement the historic structure. Traditional cabinetry is made by Mike Bell of Chicago of bleached timber from England. The women's department features a double-height ceiling that floods the space with natural light. On cloudy days, a massive custom chandelier adorned with sea creatures illuminates the area.

san francisco

architect/interior designer
FORBES SHEA

photographer
COLE HAAN

square feet/meters   3,150/293
design budget $925,000

san francisco

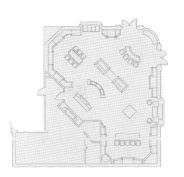

architect/interior designer
FORBES SHEA

photographer
COLE HAAN

square feet/meters   2,600/242

design budget $785,000

houston

architect/interior designer
FORBES SHEA

photographer
STEVEN FAZIO

square feet/meters   2,500/232

design budget $675,000

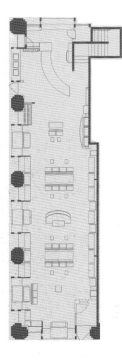

new york city

valentino

Long before Ralph, Calvin, Donna, and Tommy were fashion superstars, Valentino secured his place at the epicenter of international fashion and global licensing. Having dressed Jackie O, Liz Taylor and a host of European and American socialites, his name became perpetually synonymous with sophisticated style, sumptuous fabrics and rich detail.

Valentino knew exactly what he wanted for his Madison Avenue flagship, which opened at the end of 1997: a modern spacious boutique with an impressive double-height ceiling. He also knew exactly whom to hire: Peter Marino + Assoc Architects. Since Valentino and Marino had collaborated on two previous projects—Valentino's home in Italy and his extraordinary yacht—Valentino was confident that Marino would create an elegant store to satisfy his many requests.

The 9,300-square-foot Valentino boutique was designed to house the complete men's and women's collections, and the secondary Miss V and Oliver lines, in a visually interconnected space. Marino used large windows to reveal the impressive entry area, with its lofty ceiling and vibrant red lacquer column. Rich materials—including red lacquer, gold leaf, and a combination of light anigre and dark cerused oak—were selected to set a luxurious tone. The fashion designer's signature identity element—red lacquer—has been repeated in the logo on the walls, on the cut-out Valentino letters over the door and on various logo plaques.

Marino skillfully achieved a feeling of luxe throughout the boutique. He kept the space light and airy, as specified by Valentino, with silver-leafed ceilings, white-lacquered handbag vitrines and beige Chassagne limestone flooring in the entry area and main circulation paths. The individual clothing lines have been set apart in areas distinguished by separate color palettes, carpet and materials; flexible display shelving and casework allow for seasonal changes. For those clients unable to attend Valentino's European runway shows, video monitors were integrated within the millwork.

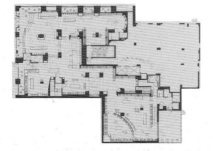

architect
PETER MARINO + ASSOC ARCHITECTS

photographer
PETER AARON

square feet/meters   9,300/864

design budget   not disclosed

baccarat

The venerable house of Baccarat has been a leading manufacturer of crystal, tabletop, vases, and jewelry for more than 200 years, selling to specialty stores worldwide. The company, which recently opened several flagship stores in the U.S., has implemented an advertising program aimed at a younger, hipper customer to support its revamped brand identity. Using a series of highly stylized images to shift the focus from tabletop to lifestyle, the ad campaign promotes the line's extensive range of gift items, decorative accessories, lighting and jewelry. The New York flagship, which showcases the entire line, is the retail component of Baccarat's new identity program.

For the Madison Avenue boutique, Jean-Pierre Heim & Associates has polished the strong, linear space. A 30-foot by 90-foot glass facade and four impressive display windows beckon passersby to enter and view the extensive display of more than 2,000 glass objects. Red carpet, a Baccarat signature, welcomes browsing customers. A striking crystal chandelier dominates the glistening atrium.

The shop's interior is encased in light sycamore walls, which complement and enhance Baccarat's shining treasures. The selling floor, divided into numerous enclaves, is defined by well-lit wood display cases, open sandblasted glass shelves and vitrines that allow for a changing display of modern and classic crystal pieces. An impressive staircase leads customers to the china department, where elegant table settings are shown on traditional wood tables and sculptured crystal pedestals.

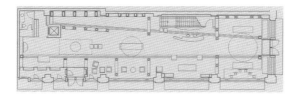

interior designer
JEAN-PIERRE HEIM & ASSOCIATES INC.

photographer
PHILIPPE L. HOUZÉ

square feet/meters   5,000/465
design budget $1.3 million

revillon

Revillon, the Paris-based luxury goods company, has been producing exquisite furs since 1723. Having recently decided to bring its opulent brand of retail to freestanding boutiques in the U.S., it has opened a posh showcase for its furs and its new collection of outerwear, rainwear, accessories and clothing. Rebecca De Vives, Revillon's president, says the stores are "for customers who want European quality and design and believe in buying established luxury brands." The stores' interiors, designed with contemporary flair by Jean-Pierre Heim, the Parisian architect and designer, are deeply rooted in French tradition.

The New York flagship, located in the Steuben Glass building on Fifth Avenue, boasts a spectacular, 100-foot floor-to-ceiling wraparound window facade into which Heim designed a series of displays depicting the imagined adventures of a Revillon traveler. Inside, the Revillon crest appears everywhere—on mirrors, wall sconces and in the cinnamon-toned Berber carpet—further establishing Revillon's prestigious retail mark and enhancing its luxury brand recognition.

Using natural materials, colors, and textures, Heim has created a dramatic shopping experience. In the New York store, an impression of soaring space is achieved by the 24-karat gold-leafed domed ceiling over the fur boutique, where vertical panels, equipped with waterfall pegs, lead the eye continually upward. Elegant fixtures add to the atmosphere. Two-tone inlaid cherry and ash cabinetry, set off by natural stone and marble, enhance the merchandise display. Curved banquettes and ceiling lines direct customers through the store and form visually distinct departments for the various collections.

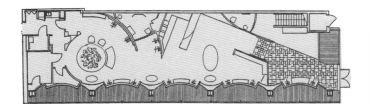

interior designer
JEAN-PIERRE HEIM & ASSOCIATES INC.

photographer
PHILIPPE L. HOUZÉ

square feet/meters   3,500/325
design budget $1.5 million

kieselstein–cord

Designer Barry Kieselstein-Cord envisioned the interior of his flagship store on prestigious Worth Avenue in Palm Beach as a luxurious shopping oasis, one that would appeal instinctively to his well-heeled international clientele. The store, which resembles a gracious salon, uniquely showcases the entire Kieselstein-Cord line of jewelry, handbags and belts, typically presented in separate areas in department stores. The 1,200-square-foot space also carries men's accessories and tabletop accessories, items only available at this location. The merchandise is displayed like fine art in a private collection or museum.

Architect Christopher Barriscale, who also served as interior designer, has adhered faithfully to Kieselstein-Cord's elegant aesthetic. He has used only the richest of materials, including limestone for the entry portal, hand-rubbed mahogany paneling, suede wallcoverings, custom carpet and Art Deco-inspired leather armchairs. Soft ambient lighting and warm neutral colors have been chosen carefully to enhance the merchandise.

The gentle curves of the walls and ceiling, wrapped in gleaming mahogany, are intended to echo the organic forms of the designer's jewelry line. In addition, they allow for a panoramic view of the entire collection. Display cases are similarly rounded for easy access. While the overall effect of the Barry Kieselstein-Cord boutique is beautifully appointed and welcoming, there is a private sales room where customers can relax in a more cloistered environment. In keeping with the retailer's approach to personalized service, soft drinks, cappuccino, even champagne, are politely offered.

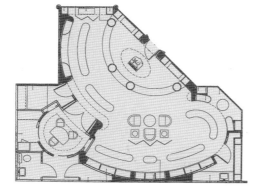

architect/interior designer
CHRISTOPHER BARRISCALE ARCHITECTS

photographer
ROSS MUIR

square feet/meters   1,200/111

design budget   not disclosed

estēe lauder

How does an established cosmetics company support its brand equity and best serve its customers' every skincare, makeup, and fragrance need? For beauty industry giant Estēe Lauder, the answer was to open its first freestanding location in Manhasset, New York. In the relaxed elegance of 5,100 square feet of open retail space, the Estēe Lauder team created a white and gold jewel box, adorned with graceful organic forms, that brings together innovative, assisted-sell merchandising with a luxurious day spa.

The focal point of the spacious entrance level is an impressive makeup area built into a central oval island. Complete with a custom color library, a popular component of many Estēe Lauder counters across North America, this ultimate merchandising tool is a makeup playground where a comprehensive range of color lies within easy reach of each customer. Here, shoppers are invited to browse, touch and sample hundreds of makeup shades.

Within Estēe Lauder's gleaming retail space is a lavish spa, a tranquil oasis where customers can drop in for a few moments of pampering or indulge in a day of head-to-toe beauty services. Luxury materials—lacewood, marble, and platinum and gold leaf—reiterate the company's image.

Throughout the Estēe Lauder Store and Spa, compelling lifestyle marketing encourages customers to make a purchase because it makes them feel good. The Lauder imprint is found everywhere—from recognizable photographs suspended from a metal cable system in the full-height glass storefront to the blue packaging so familiar to generations of customers.

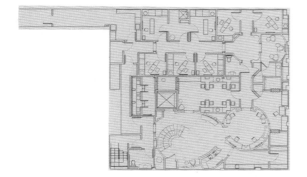

architect/interior designer
ESTĒE LAUDER STORE DESIGN

photographer
FREDERICK CHARLES

square feet/meters   5,100/474

design budget   not disclosed

lipton

When the Thomas J. Lipton Co., one of the world's most recognized consumer brands, decided to expand its wholesale business into a retail format, it summoned the design firm Donovan and Green to create the Lipton Teahouse in Old Pasadena, California. As a prototype for a potential 200 shops to be built nationwide, the client dictated the creation of an image that was disinctly different from Lipton's well-known supermarket packaging but that retained the familiarity of the venerable red-and-white label. Donovan and Green not only created the architectural design, but it also developed a total concept for a new brand identity. Driving the design was the "whole notion of a quality tea experience," explained firm principal, Nancye Green. To create a new aesthetic, the designers developed a new logo. They then applied it to everything from signage and packaging to uniforms and serviceware.

Intended to convey both the invigorating and relaxing qualities of tea, the first Lipton Teahouse was conceived as a narrow, deep space that reflects the intense greens of the tea leaf and warm amber tones of brewed tea. The front of the store was arranged to include semicircular counter space, window counters and open shelves for boxed teas and tea paraphernalia. Parlorlike tables and banquettes were installed in the rear, inviting guests to linger over pots of brewed teas, including new herbal blends. The picture rail display of 30 historical photographs from Lipton's archives was created to add visual interest.

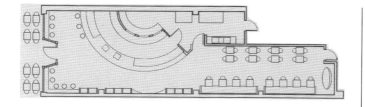

architect/interior designer
DONOVAN AND GREEN

photographer
JIM HEDRICH

square feet/meters   2,800/260

design budget $300,000

lacoste

Mention the phrase "logo shirt," and Lacoste comes immediately to mind as the brand that started it all. The familiar green crocodile has been gracing pique knit shirts since its founder, tennis champion René Lacoste, started the company 65 years ago.

Today, the Lacoste company is a complete line of men's, women's, and children's sportswear and accessories, each identified by classic, sporty styling and the famous crocodile logo. With established brand recognition and worldwide wholesale distribution, it makes good business sense to take the company to the next level: freestanding stores. The Lacoste boutique in the Forum Shops at Caesar's in Las Vegas is an outstanding example of brand building through visual merchandising.

A unique focal point of the new boutique in Las Vegas is a giant three-dimensional crocodile, mounted on a world map that pinpoints all U.S. Lacoste retail locations and the Paris corporate headquarters. Below the map, products are hung and shelved on movable wall fixtures that blend with the shop's classic, neutral palette. The newest Lacoste boutiques, such as this one, also feature a "color wall"—changeable spools of yarn from the Troyes, France, mill that showcase the 40 colors in which Lacoste pique shirts are available each season. Lacoste's extensive color range is also portrayed on shiny white shopping bags that picture a stack of pique shirts in varied tones.

Throughout the customer-friendly 1,700-square-foot boutique, brand equity is reinforced through subtle details bearing the Lacoste signature—the crocodile logo is repeated in matte silver ornamenting wood hangers, on the matte metal coins ornamenting all fixtures and on the wide brushed-chrome band around the cash-wrap desk.

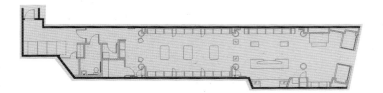

architect
FORBES SHEA

photographer
ROBERT WALKER

square feet/meters   1,700/158

design budget   not disclosed

giorgio armani

Among today's fashion leaders, no name is more synonymous with luxurious fabrics, muted neutrals, impeccable tailoring and clean classic designs than Giorgio Armani. His enduring style has influenced the way women and men dress for the last quarter of this century. With sophisticated self-assurance, and elegant, understated designs, Armani has expanded his label into one of the world's most successful retail empires. Armani has established worldwide strongholds for his multiple divisions. None interprets the company's refined elegance so purely as its premier Giorgio Armani boutiques.

When Giorgio Armani opened his eighth U.S. boutique at the prestigious Bal Harbour Shops, he worked closely with New York-based architect S. Russell Groves to create a space that is the architectural equivalent of his sophisticated fashions. Housing the Black Label ready-to-wear and accessories collections, as well as Giorgio Armani Golf and Giorgio Armani Neve, the 4,000-square-foot store reflects the sun-washed tones and light textures of its Florida locale. Groves has framed the storefront using pale limestone plinths and large glass windows to set a stage for what is inside. Full-height frosted-glass panels define the various men's and women's collections, providing an ethereal flow from one niche to another.

Throughout this Giorgio Armani boutique, neutral tones add a subtle quality to the merchandise presentation. Groves clad the walls in whitewashed Venetian plaster, anchoring them with deep brown concrete floors and sisal area rugs. Freestanding vitrines of pale American ash hold folded items while a flexible stainless-steel hangbar system displays hanging merchandise. Silver-leafed panels serve as a backdrop for display faceouts and hide back stock. To endow the space with a warm glow, the architect has used diffused lighting hidden throughout the boutique. Back-lit frosted panels and display niches are washed with light.

architect
S. RUSSELL GROVES

photographer
PETER MAUSS

square feet/meter   4,000/372

design budget   not disclosed

salvatore ferragamo

Some of the world's most glamorous people have worn Ferragamo shoes. The prestigious Florentine retailer established its reputation by producing the finest Italian leather goods; today, the Ferragamo name is a recognized brand with numerous product lines that epitomize sophistication and elegance. So too does its North American headquarters on Fifth Avenue in New York City.

The women's store, located at 663 Fifth Avenue, occupies 5,534 square feet of ground-floor retail space. The 2,481-square-foot men's retail area is located on the main level next door at Trump Tower. Both shops were co-designed by architects Kenne Shepherd, of New York, and Roberto Monsani, of Florence, so that they would be consistent with each other as well as with other Ferragamo shops worldwide. Each features a full range of men's and women's Ferragamo products.

Faithful to Ferragamo's clean sophisticated style, the architects adopted a minimalist approach for stores' interiors. The retail areas are layed out in a series of rooms, the largest of which is the shoe salon. Other rooms are dedicated to handbags, briefcases and luggage, ladies' and men's wear and accessories. Although separate and partially enclosed, each area flows easily into the next. All merchandise is displayed against beige lacquered panels surrounded by black lacquered frames. Handbags and shoes are presented on fabric-wrapped shelves outlined in a bleached cherry wood frame. Photomurals and lighting distinguish the separate product areas.

The architects paid special attention to illuminating the stores uniformly. Lighting is provided under the shelves and at the top of the wall display fixtures. General ambient light is also created by uplighting, available from custom designed light fixtures suspended from the ceiling. This device essentially opens up the store. Spotlights on the bottom side of the hanging fixtures highlight displayed merchandise below.

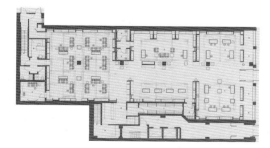

architects/interior designers
KENNE SHEPHERD INTERIOR
DESIGN·ARCHITECTURE PLLC
STUDIO MONSANI

photographer
TOSHI YOSHIMI

square feet/meters   12,533/1,164

design budget   not disclosed

fifth avenue

fifth avenue

architects/interior designers
**KENNE SHEPHERD INTERIOR
DESIGN·ARCHITECTURE PLLC**
STUDIO MONSANI

photographer
TOSHI YOSHIMI

square feet/meters   4,681/435

design budget   not disclosed

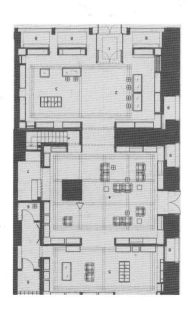

trump tower

polo ralph lauren

In the 31 years since Ralph Lauren established the Polo label, he has revolutionized the fashion industry by developing a visionary concept of lifestyle merchandising. His distinctive and powerful approach to advertising, interior design and retailing has made Polo one of the most successful consumer brands in the world.

Polo's reputation and romantic American image have been developed across an ever-expanding number of products, brands and international markets. Today, Ralph Lauren's domain includes men's, women's and children's apparel, accessories, home furnishings and fragrances.

Mr. Lauren's desire to showcase his world in an exquisitely designed environment set new standards in retailing. In 1971, the designer was the first American to open a free-standing retail store, in Beverly Hills. Ten years later, he was the first American designer to open a European retail outlet in London. His New York flagship store in the Rhinelander mansion on Madison Avenue, which opened in 1986, enabled him to create a total environment using a collection of products that celebrates the best of American taste and style.

There are now 40 freestanding stores in the United States and 76 stores in 27 other countries. The company's products are also sold in leading department stores, where Mr. Lauren pioneered the shop-within-shop boutique dedicated exclusively to one designer. Today there are more than 4,500 Polo Ralph Lauren shop-within-shop boutiques worldwide.

To assist with the architectural planning of freestanding Ralph Lauren stores in the United States, the designer turned to leading architectural and interior design firms across the country. Yet, with more than 100 locations worldwide, the interior vision of each Ralph Lauren store presents a consistent concept. His signature retail interiors are rich in highly polished wood cabinetry, sisal or Persian rugs, crackled leather or overstuffed upholstered armchairs, beautifully framed photographs and antique accessories.

In 1998, Polo Ralph Lauren opened its first freestanding children's shop, adjacent to a new Polo Sport store in Manhasset, New York. These additions, plus a recently enlarged Polo Ralph Lauren store, were under the direction of Peter Marino + Assoc Architects. The interior design of the children's shop was by Polo Store Development in conjunction with James Harb Architects and Naomi Leff and Associates.

Backen Arrigoni & Ross, San Francisco architects, were hired to design the Polo Ralph Lauren store in Phoenix, which opened in 1997. The interior styling is by Polo Store Development.

phoenix

architect
BACKEN ARRIGONI & ROSS

interior designer
POLO STORE DEVELOPMENT

photographer
RICKY ZEHAVI

square feet/meters   12,700/1,180

design budget   not disclosed

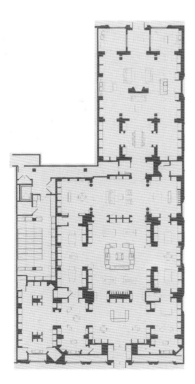

phoenix

manhasset

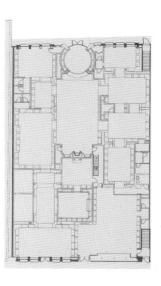

architect
PETER MARINO + ASSOC ARCHITECTS

interior designers
JAMES HARB ARCHITECTS
NAOMI LEFF AND ASSOCIATES
POLO STORE DEVELOPMENT

photographer
RICKY ZEHAVI

square feet/meters   27,000/2,508

design budget   not disclosed

anne klein

The Anne Klein Company has been linked to elegant American style since its innovative designer's mid-century emergence as the creator of coordinated designer separates. Although Ms. Klein is no longer alive, and the original upper-end collection is on hiatus, her legacy lives on in the Anne Klein Company, an updated, multi-division resource for bridge departments. Offering stylish day and evening clothing at affordable prices and lucrative licensing potential, the company has broad wholesale distribution, as well as successful retail outposts in Asia, South America, and the Middle East. To create greater name recognition in the United States, and to present all ready-to-wear and accessories lines within a single venue, the Anne Klein Company opened its first freestanding Anne Klein store at the Ala Moana Center in Honolulu, Hawaii.

Charles Lau and Robert Domingo, of AM Partners, Inc., chose pale woods and light floors and walls as neutral backdrops for the Anne Klein merchandise. Paul Bennett, of Bennett Lowry Corporation, created mannequin vignettes and display cases that show how the various components of the collections work together. A luxurious touch is an intimate seating area, toward the rear of the store near the dressing rooms. Here, customers and their companions can enjoy refreshments while viewing videos of current collections.

The entire Anne Klein collection—apparel, shoes, handbags, small leather goods, belts, watches, sunglasses, swimwear and scarves—takes center stage throughout the subdued, 4,500-square-foot boutique. Visuals from the current season's advertising campaign prominently support the Anne Klein brand.

architects
AM PARTNERS, INC.
BENNETT LOWRY CORPORATION

interior designer
BENNETT LOWRY CORPORATION

photographer
GARY HOFHEIMER PHOTOGRAPHY

square feet/meters   4,500/418

design budget $959,000

chanel

The house of Chanel, synonymous with classic modern elegance, has endowed its jewel of a flagship on East 57th Street in New York with signature refinement. The 17-story glass-and-granite structure, designed by the New York architectural firm Platt Byard Dovell, features black granite trim that recalls the black borders of Chanel's distinct packaging.

The 7,000-square-foot Chanel boutique, which occupies the first two floors, is a study in sophistication. Designed by Brand + Allen Architecture, of San Francisco, and Christian Gallion, of Paris, the interior boasts a subtle palette of black lacquer, beige stone and mirrors inspired by the Chanel Boutique at 31 Rue Cambon in Paris. In fact, the design concept for Chanel Boutiques worldwide retains a consistent palette faithful to the deep rooted image of Chanel.

The New York flagship accentuates luxury—from choice of materials to spacious comfortable fitting rooms. Noteworthy is the 3,000-square-foot third-floor salon created for fashion shows and special events, and outfitted to resemble Coco Chanel's famed apartment above her atelier.

Numerous details ensure visitors a shopping experience that reflects the venerable heritage of Chanel. Wide glass doors, opened by a smartly uniformed doorman, feature unique octagonal glass doorknobs modeled after the famous Chanel No. 5 perfume-bottle stopper. The signature octagon is repeated in the shape of the entrance foyer as well as on its creamy French limestone floor.

A double staircase with intricate wrought-iron railings is designed as an architectural salute to the famous Rue Cambon mirrored staircase. It leads to the second level, which presents the complete Chanel ready-to-wear collection. On the same floor, overlooking 57th Street, is Chanel's jewelry boutique.

Chanel's Fine Jewellery Boutique on the Place Vendome in Paris reopened in 1998 after a year of meticulous renovation. The building in which it is located was purchased by Coco Chanel in the 1930s. Already listed as a national historical treasure, it covers an area of some 200 square meters. Customers gain access via a carriage entrance with restored blue wood doors dating from 1699, the year the façade of "18 Place Vendome" was erected.

new york

new york

new york

architect
PLATT BYARD DOVELL ARCHITECTS

interior designer
BRAND + ALLEN ARCHITECTS, INC.

photographer
NORMAN McGRATH

square feet/meters   10,000/929

design budget   not disclosed

paris

architect/interior designer
CHRISTIAN GALLION

photographer
CHANEL

square feet/meters   2,153/200

design budget   not disclosed

millennium

MIX

dolce & gabbana

Domenico Dolce and Stefano Gabbana are internationally acclaimed for their hip, sensuous clothing designs, inspired by sexy Italian film stars of the 1950s and by their native Sicily. They opened their first American flagship on Madison Avenue in New York in 1997. It features the full men's and women's apparel and accessories collections plus fragrances.

The 7,000-square-foot store was designed by Florentine architect Claudio Nardi in the spirit of the original Milan boutique, which combines traditional baroque elements within a modern frame. Milanese designer Rodolfo Dordoni contributed the interior, which, true to the Dolce & Gabbana design aesthetic, captures the essence of sophisticated modern Italy and at the same time respects its traditions.

The New York store has been used as the protoype for Dolce & Gabbana boutiques around the globe, part of a concerted effort to control the image of the brand. Architect Nardi and designer Dordoni used Chiarabell limestone for the floor and painted the walls with a soft white *spazzolato* swirled-paint technique. Two large, ornate mirrors and accent walls covered in cranberry red silk hint subtly at the designers' Italian heritage.

The architectural focal point of the flagship is the glass-walled garden filled with hand-painted clay pots and plants indigenous to the Sicilian countryside. The designers, who have attracted a strong Hollywood following, have installed a VIP room on the second floor, just off the garden.

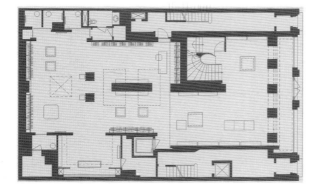

architect
CLAUDIO NARDI ARCHITETTO

interior designer
STUDIO DORDONI

photographer
TODD EBERLE

square feet/meters   7,000/650

design budget   not disclosed

shu uemura

SoHo, the historic Manhattan neighborhood filled with cast-iron industrial buildings, has been home to artists' lofts and galleries for the last three decades. But today, as galleries move out and a bevy of single-brand stores move in, the new art is beauty and the new galleries are loft-like outlets for beauty brands. Individual cosmetics lines have emerged from crowded department store counters to create visual excitement in spare, non-aggressive environments of their own.

Shu Uemura, the celebrated Japanese makeup artist, has created a line of makeup, brushes and skin care products that sells in exclusive specialty stores like Barneys New York. He has also opened the Shu Uemura Beauty Boutique on Greene Street, SoHo, in a prewar industrial building. Designed by Satoru Hamamura of Spasso Environment Planning, Inc., Tokyo, this modern space artfully blends the structure's architectural integrity with an atmosphere of humanity, hospitality and elegance.

The challenge for the architect Hamamura, who worked with the New York-based design firm Matsuyama International Corporation, was to enhance the 24-foot by 100-foot tunnel-like space and create a way for traffic to flow from the open-sell store front through the clear glass wall to the semi-private makeup room in the rear. Keeping it neat and clean, the designer has used off-white lacquer finishes and baked-paint coatings on cabinet surfaces and display cases. Other units sport butcher block and stained bird's-eye maple. To soften the hard lines of the envelope and downplay the height of the 14-foot ceiling, the architect added sheetrock-over-plywood curvatures that he calls "ceiling dividers." Circular patterns have been used throughout the space to showcase Shu Uemura's signature beauty cycle.

In the serene studio-like Shu Uemura Beauty Boutique, the product speaks for itself. Stock is organized in clear acrylic display cases and cylinders. Makeup tools are arranged like precise Ikebana designs. A unique feature of the boutique is a set of light simulation boxes, where customers test makeup colors in a variety of lighting conditions.

architect
SPASSO ENVIRONMENT PLANNING, INC.

interior designers
MATSUYAMA INTERNATIONAL CORPORATION
SPASSO ENVIRONMENT PLANNING, INC.

photographer
PAUL WARCHOL

square feet/meters   1,368/127

design budget $500,000

emporio armani

Giorgio Armani's signature refinement can be found wherever his name appears—in his merchandise, in his advertising, and especially in his boutiques, where his philosophy and creative energy permeate everything from the clothing on the racks to the design and construction of the space. Armani has remained true to his identity throughout the multiple divisions of his company by creating successful prototypes for the stores as well as the brands— the Emporio Armani boutiques, selling the secondary line of men's and women's wear, accessories and home designs, not excepted.

When Mr. Armani decided to establish a meaningful retail presence in Canada, he chose S. Russell Groves to launch a new design direction for the Emporio Armani division. His first outpost, in Toronto, is a block-long building on Bloor Street surrounded by high profile neighbors such as Holt Renfrew, a partner in the Armani project. The prolific designer and his talented architect envisioned a space that was very clean, very modern, and very light. A cantilevered canopy with prominent signage greets customers. For visual interest, Groves broke through the ground level's ceiling slab, creating a double-height space topped by a canted skylight. The familiar Giorgio Armani eagle is projected onto a large wall at the skylight. To balance the subdued linear quality of the space, Groves subtly curved the painted metal, limestone and glass stairway, and added rounded ceiling lines.

Throughout the 7,000-square-foot boutique, fixtures of richly textured light wood offset the shop's refined environment. Concealed lighting endows the space with a warm glow. Designed for optimum flexibility, the backlit modular system adapts to double or single rows for face-out or side-hanging merchandise, or shelves for folded items. Custom display cubes can be placed in rows or stacked with changeable pegs and dowels. Long freestanding tables hold removable storage containers. Seamlessly integrated with the selling space is a limestone-clad coffee bar and adjacent seating area with rift-cut oak furnishings.

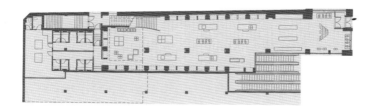

architect
S. RUSSELL GROVES

photographer
VOLKER SEDING

square feet/meters   7,000/650

design budget   not disclosed

philosophy di alberta ferretti

Italian designer Alberta Ferretti is best known for sophisticated slip dresses made with delicate, romantic fabrics. Her fashions, while seemingly minimalist, are delicate multi-layered garments much sought after for their ethereal, dramatic styling.

When the designer decided to open her first freestanding boutique in the United States to present her Philosophy Collection, she selected New York architect David Ling, who transformed a 1,000-square-foot Federal-style townhouse in SoHo into an "illuminated Renaissance theater." His goal was to create a multi-layered architectural setting echoing the fashion designer's gauzy creations. The resulting renovation, unlike any other fashion boutique in the neighborhood, is revealed completely behind a three-story glass storefront. Flooded with natural and artificial light, the shop is indeed an exciting theatrical showcase.

The architect completely gutted the building and built two loft-like floors behind a newly constructed brick wall, which he washed in metallic aluminum paint. He also installed two vertical four-story skylit shafts, one by the front window and one by the sandblasted glass rear wall and main stairwell. This clever architectural device allows the mezzanine level to float seemingly between the two illuminated shafts. The layered effect also enables the space to appear larger than it is in reality. Echoing Ferretti's airy slip dresses, Ling also layered the geometric staircase with a sheer cotton scrim hung from ceiling mounted stainless-steel rods. Ling's choices for architectural finishes—hand-burnished mother-of-pearl walls, acid-washed poured concrete floors and sanded stainless-steel display fixtures—also relate to the fashion designer's preference for textural contrasts. Three bold geometric forms—the curvilinear cash wrap, wavy partition and a massive ornamental piece suspended from the ceiling over the front of the store—are sculptural elements that accentuate the geometry of the architecture.

architect/interior designer
DAVID LING ARCHITECTS

photographer
© 1998 TODD EBERLE

square feet/meters   1,000/93

design budget   not disclosed

ghost

Flirty, colorful, and diaphanous are words associated with Ghost, the 15-year-old label designed and run by Tanya Sarne. To raise the visibility of the collection beyond its British base, this contemporary women's wear company has recently opened stores in Paris and Los Angeles, its first two freestanding locations outside of England. Designed by Ted Walters of Walters London Ltd., both shops convey the Ghost philosophy by echoing the soft and varied textures of the merchandise in the interior surfaces.

The first new installation, on Rue Montmartre in the heart of Paris, is a boutique in the true sense. The structure's 1,200-square-foot envelope forms a striking backdrop to the collection, which is hung simply along one long wall. Polished stained-wood floors and a circular cash wrap desk contrast with gleaming white walls to give the boutique a sense of spaciousness.

With a specialty store business already established in California, and a style suited to relaxed Los Angeles sensibilities, Ms. Sarne has opened her first U.S. Ghost flagship on fashionable North Robertson Boulevard. Significantly larger than the Paris boutique, the 3,500-square-foot interior in Los Angeles houses a full range of merchandise—women's separates, shoes, scarves, a small men's collection, home accessories and a coordinating line of jewelry by Erickson Beamon—in a complete environment that captures and elevates Ghost's brand identity. With deft minimalism, Walters has designed a system that reflects seasonal changes in daylight and uses sliding acrylic screens over the store windows.

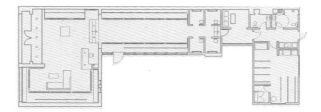

interior designer
WALTERS LONDON LTD.

photographer
EDMUND A. BARR

square feet/meters   3,500/325

design budget $500,000

los angeles

los angeles

interior designer
WALTERS LONDON LTD.

photographer
PAUL MAURER

square feet/meters   1,200/111

design budget $250,000

paris

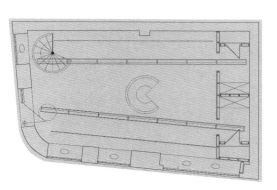

laundry by shelli segal

When architect Michael Neumann was commissioned to design the first freestanding store for Laundry by Shelli Segal in SoHo, he took his cue from the clean lines of Ms. Segal's sexy, contemporary body-conscious dress and sportswear collection. Neumann's spare, easily adaptable floor plan and materials' palette now appear right in sync with Laundry's well-edited, modern philosophy.

Intended to complement and showcase the clothing, the architecture intentionally emphasizes the raw beauty of natural and man-made materials. Neumann deftly juxtaposes flooring of synthetic poured concrete against soft suede-like upholstery and mesh stainless-steel fitting room curtains. For a luxurious touch, he has stuffed the club chairs with down, installed ebonized mahogany cabinetry and used only satin nickel hardware. A perimeter wall system provides for flexible display. The surface features a single outfit hanging from a satin nickel puck; adjacent openings punched into the wall contain adjustable shelving and nickel handrods.

Since its inception, Laundry by Shelli Segal has maintained such a high level of success that the company now verges on big-brand status. The overall effect of its new flagship is clean and contemporary. The design is easily adaptable to the growing numbers of in-store shops employing the same display elements and poured concrete flooring.

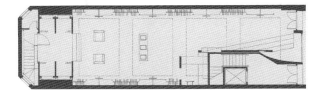

architect/interior designer
MICHAEL NEUMANN ARCHITECTURE

photographer
© MARK ROSS 1998

square feet/meters   2,000/186

design budget   not disclosed

eileen fisher

Eileen Fisher's minimalist clothing conveys a sense of ease and understated elegance for the contemporary woman. Within a relatively short time, the company has developed a loyal following through major department and specialty stores, as well as a growing number of freestanding boutiques in select cities and fashion malls.

Working closely with Fisher, Lea Cloud and Victoria Rospond of CR Studio, Architects PC, planned the 4,000-square-foot Eileen Fisher SoHo flagship as a prototype for new installations. Here, Ms. Fisher's design philosophy is established in an architectural language that reflects the simplicity and systematic layering of her clothing. The architects employed a cohesive set of materials selected for their inherent richness and tactile qualities. The interior consists of two central spaces, a main 3,000-square-foot loft-like area, and an adjacent 1,000-square-foot room that houses a higher-end line.

To allow for flexibility and seasonal changes, two design strategies were implemented. First, a long pocket wall and fixed perimeter hanging are used to display a continuum of seasonal silhouettes. Second, movable fixtures and tables allow for variations in merchandising techniques, grouping the Eileen Fisher coordinated separates. Large skylights flood the interior with natural light.

A unique feature of the SoHo flagship signifies Eileen Fisher's corporate philosophy of giving back to the community. A steel canopy wraps the corner back into a 12-foot by 30-foot Zen-like garden space, tripling the storefront display area and creating an intriguing entry. Providing a tranquil moment of relief from the cityscape, the garden is lined in granite pavers with Mexican beach stones, and contains a stainless-steel trellis, bronze fountain, cedar wall and bench, and charming crab apple tree.

Because of its generous space and upgraded custom fixtures, the new SoHo flagship most closely reflects Eileen Fisher's design aesthetic. Subtle materials, signage and a carefully articulated combination of natural and artificial light, softened by panels of translucent ceiling scrim, act as support for the quality of the clothing and accessories.

architect/interior designer
CR STUDIO, ARCHITECTS PC

photographer
PAUL WARCHOL

square feet/meters   4,000/372

design budget $1.5 million

max studio

The trendy Fashion Island Mall in Newport Beach, California, is the setting for Max Studio's prototype store, which was designed in 1997 by the innovative California-based architecture firm of Shubin + Donaldson in collaboration with interior designer Jim Lassiter. Max Studio, a women's clothing line known for its casual elegance, quality fabrics and affordability, was seeking to establish a consistent architectural statement for future retail openings. In keeping with the contemporary style of the clothing, the designers have created a clean, stylishly minimal setting to showcase the apparel. This theme is carried out in department store boutiques as well.

There are no distractions from the shopping experience. The spatial aesthetic is a study in simplicity. Materials are natural and kept to a minimum. The architects have selected indirect lighting that casts soft shadows on the subtle lines of the clothes and shades of the Max Studio palette. Display cases and flooring are made of a light maple intended to contrast with wrought-iron rod holders and mannequin bases. A towering screen looks like a contemporary sculpture and cleverly separates the front of the store from the dressing room area. It also functions as a mirror on the reverse. Functional and artistic, the screen underscores the ambiance of a contemporary gallery.

To maximize its appearance from the mall, Shubin + Donaldson have installed a massive, seemingly transparent display window which allows customers unencumbered views of the merchandise. Two over-sized door handles provide the only clue that shoppers are separated from the interior.

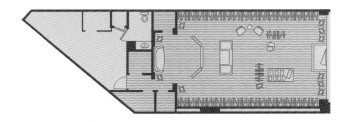

architect
SHUBIN + DONALDSON ARCHITECTS

interior designer
JIM LASSITER & COMPANY

photographer
JOHN M. FORD

square feet/meters   1,100/102

design budget $82,500

bcbg max azria

Bon Chic, Bon Genre—French slang for good style, good attitude—captures the inventive spirit of BCBG Max Azria's design and merchandising philosophy. In just ten years, this leading contemporary women's clothing and accessories company has become a major department and specialty store resource and built a network of company-owned freestanding stores throughout North America and the world. The newest and largest BCBG Max Azria, a 6,300-square-foot flagship in Washington, D.C.'s historic Georgetown district, reflects the sleek signature modernity of this contemporary lifestyle brand.

The boutique, a centuries-old firehouse and barn linked by a newly enclosed skylit courtyard, houses all the BCBG Max Azria divisions—sportswear, dresses, jeans, swimwear, accessories and footwear. While the exterior remains intact, the inside space has been reinterpreted and updated with modern sophistication, design and technology by Steven Vanze of Barnes & Vanze & Associates and the BCBG design team of Nathalie Ryan and owner Max Azria. The landmarked four-story building has been converted to two spacious levels with soaring 20-foot ceilings that enhance the sophisticated, pared-down style of BCBG's separates and collections. Entering the store through its original oversized mahogany doors, customers encounter crisp white walls, recessed lighting and a graceful cantilevered central staircase.

Part of the overwhelming strength of BCBG is its ability to communicate with customers through its stores. To convey BCBG's sexy young message, wall-mounted TV monitors play videos of the current season's runway shows, images from advertising campaigns grace the walls and stylized mannequins showcase key looks. Individual collections are clearly arranged in departments created by engaging nooks and alcoves that flow through the space. Throughout the store, BCBG's brand identity is further enhanced through maple logo hangers that coordinate with handsome maple and brushed-nickel fixtures.

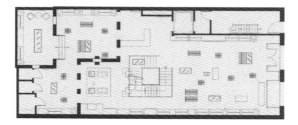

architects
BARNES & VANZE & ASSOCIATES
BCBG MAX AZRIA

interior designer
BCBG MAX AZRIA

photographer
KATHLEEN BEALL

square feet/meters   6,300/585

design budget   not disclosed

a|x
armani exchange

When the three-ton, 32-foot-high sliding stainless-steel door on the corner of Manhattan's Fifth Avenue and 51st Street opened in 1998, it heralded the arrival of A|X Armani Exchange. The 10,000-square-foot flagship, the company's largest, established a sophisticated new design prototype for the chain. Architect Keith Hobb, of London-based United Designers, worked closely with Giorgio Armani. To ensure that the two-level store reflected Armani's personal preferences and fashion philosophy, Hobb chose to line the simple volume with unexpectedly elegant materials.

Since its inception in 1991, the A|X line has evolved into a well-rounded, versatile collection of men's and women's jeans and casual clothes that mixes seasonal fashion items with redefined basics—Armani-style. Inspired by Italy's open-air markets, the A|X Armani Exchange store design reflects a utilitarian sensibility. Floor-to-ceiling windows and abundant lighting help reinforce a feeling of outdoors; simple, custom fixtures of brushed wood and stainless steel contain folded merchandise, recalling a self-service market. High vaulted ceilings, composed of two layers of metal—perforated aluminum underneath corrugated steel—are well-lit, providing an unusual diaphanous effect.

To the rear of the street floor of A|X Armani Exchange, a 20-foot-wide panel swivels to feature images from the current print campaign and draws traffic to the wrap desk. A sleek staircase with stainless-steel balustrade moves customers to the store's lower level. Shoppers can also descend via a large glass elevator encased in green-glazed ceramic tile. Throughout the shop, sandstone floors echo time-worn cobblestone streets of Italy.

A|X Armani Exchange may be the most casual and least expensive of all the company's lines, but the spacious store and its relaxed merchandise exhibit the plain elegance that is unmistakably Armani.

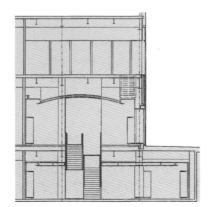

architect/interior designer
UNITED DESIGNERS

photographer
JAMES LATTANZIO

square feet/meters   10,000/929

design budget   not disclosed

dkny

In Donna Karan's own words, her secondary line, DKNY, has always been inspired by "the energy [and] individuality…that pulsates along the streets of New York." With a well-established retail base and growing numbers of international DKNY freestanding stores, it is no wonder that her edgy, urban sophistication is as recognized worldwide as it is in Manhattan.

Designed by New York architect Paul Bennett, of Bennett Lowry Corporation, the Berlin boutique is located in a visually active through-block shopping galleria bedecked with bold patterned flooring and walls. Conceived as a calm balance to its busy exterior space, DKNY Berlin offers customers a single serene shop in which to enter the designer's complete brand environment. All divisions of DKNY come together under one roof in minimally separated rooms and product presentations.

The total DKNY brand makes up a spatial, material and graphic aesthetic that has inspired Lowry with design direction. He has developed a neutral space that enhances the brand's point of view. An open storefront creates a visible sweep that immediately reveals all that the store offers. Exposed ceilings, ductwork, clothing fixtures and lighting convey the DKNY energy without obstructing its minimalist mood. Stainless-steel rods drop from the ceiling for hanging merchandise and thick white-lacquered slabs form the base for table presentations.

To unify areas of individual merchandise categories, the architect has used the ceiling plane over the center of the shop. This shiny white-lacquered form directs the flow of movement and sight lines through the store in a race track fashion, providing subconscious shifts from circulation areas to dedicated space to the products. Reinforcing the urban attitude of DKNY Berlin, high-voltage music coordinates with multiple video walls to further enhance brand imagery.

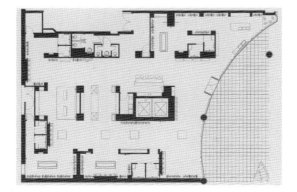

architect
BENNETT LOWRY CORPORATION

photographer
ANGELIKA KOHLMEIER

square feet/meters   5,350/497

design budget   not disclosed

calvin klein

Calvin Klein searched for many years until he found the perfect location and space for a flagship store that would promote the totality of the Calvin Klein identity. It was worth the wait. His 20,000-square-foot showcase, replete with 20-foot ceilings and triple-height windows, displays the essence of his sensuous modern style. The structure, formerly home to the venerable JP Morgan Bank, is situated at Madison Avenue and 60th Street, the epicenter of one of the world's most prestigious shopping areas. Says Klein: "The store presents a distillation of clean, spare luxury, a space in which every element, from the clothes to the architecture, reflects the same spirit."

Calvin Klein chose British architect John Pawson, known for designing art galleries in New York and London, to renovate the structure because the two share a minimalist aesthetic. Collaborating with New York architect Kenne Shepherd, they created an architecturally memorable space to serve as a neutral background for the merchandise. The full Calvin Klein women's collection—clothing, handbags, shoes, scarves, belts, eyewear and jewelry—is presented on the first floor, making it easy to accessorize. Fragrances, bridal registry and the home collection are located on the lower level. The second floor is devoted to men's wear. Evening wear is showcased by itself on the mezzanine.

The success of the Calvin Klein flagship emanates from its unique combination of flawless minimalism with maximum luxury. The façade of the distinguished building remains visually unchanged except for panels of glass three-stories high. Inside, the architecture creates an impressive yet serene statement, highlighting the entire Calvin Klein Collection without distraction.

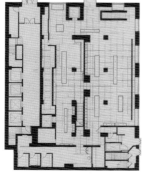

ground floor

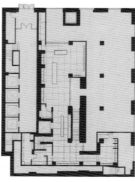

mezzanine

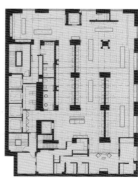

second floor

architects
KENNE SHEPHERD INTERIOR
DESIGN·ARCHITECTURE PLLC
JOHN PAWSON

interior designer
JOHN PAWSON

photographer
TODD EBERLE

square feet/meters   20,000/1,858

design budget   not disclosed

now

VOYAGERS

swatch

In the heart of New York City's 57th Street retail zone lies the Swatch Timeship. The Swiss watchmaker's 5,400-square-foot flagship is a dynamic design that reflects the watches' mechanical precision and visual creativity. The store presents a unique shopping environment based on an idea that nothing renders time more accurately than movement, a program developed by Pentagram Design in 1996.

Says Yann Gamard, president of the Swatch Group's U.S. operations: "People recognize that we aren't just a fashion brand, but also a high-tech brand." The flagship in New York, a Paris store that opened in the summer of 1997 and the 250 franchised Swatch stores worldwide are about "taking retail into our own hands. We are not just presenting a product, but a whole atmosphere."

The Swatch Timeship in New York is dominated by a storefront window that represents a mammoth Swatch model GK209 ("Jelly"), a giant timepiece measuring over 12½ feet in diameter. The building façade is clad in bright blue rigidized metal, a type of stainless steel.

Pentagram has carried dramatic visual elements through the interior design. Watches are displayed on the main retail level in a glass vacuum, or pneumatic tube system, which interconnects the three distinctive floors. The sense of motion is reinforced by using transparent and reflective materials such as mirrors and burnished aluminum, as well as changing video images and lighting installations.

On the ground floor is the Club Chamber, a double-height area with a blue terrazzo floor and a collectors' wall display of classic Swatch designs. Special promotional events are held here. On the mezzanine level lies the home of Dr. Swatch, the repair center. Customers are encouraged to sit on stools and watch video monitors telling the story of manufacturing Swatch parts and components. The third floor is a gallery, where the work of artistic collaborators such as Keith Haring, Annie Liebowitz and Yoko Ono have been exhibited. Also located here is the Swatch Bar, where customers order from a selection of watches and beverages. Flickering digital numbers on walls announce the arrival of watches as they enter through the tube system.

This shopping experience is at once high tech, interactive and fun.

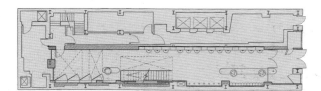

architect/interior designer
PENTAGRAM DESIGN INC

photographer
DUB ROGERS

square feet/meters   5,400/502

design budget   not disclosed

fossil

The clean white box that Fossil selected for its retail shop in the Tuttle Crossing Mall in Columbus, Ohio has provided JGA, Inc with free rein to create an environment that enhances its established brand identity. Fossil's hip, retro-style watches and accessories sparked the idea for a stylized vintage '50s theme. The design firm has given Fossil a fresh example of contemporary retro, a strong visual aesthetic built on a fusion of nostalgic references and modern style elements.

At the entrance, the honey toned maple-veneered wrap of the storefront curves into a double door featuring Fossil's mosaic logo in the tile threshold. A neon clock, '50s-style gas pump and vintage advertising logos from the company's vast archives punctuate the front of the store, visually reiterating the brand vocabulary. Crowning the sleek interior, with its warm ecru palette and cherry and maple veneers, is a smooth ceiling with simple dropped soffits, recessed lighting and point spots interrupted by a wedge of traditional tin ceiling tiles.

The deep, narrow space of Fossil's 2,800-square-foot store has been conceived as a fluid passageway with handsome round-cornered fixtures clad in maple, cherry and glass. The graceful curve of the watch display encourages shoppers to move from the storefront into the shop, where a prominent display wall of sunglasses enhanced by nostalgic advertising posters beckons shoppers to the back of the store. Accessories and leather goods are tastefully arranged on sleek, stained-wood nesting tables.

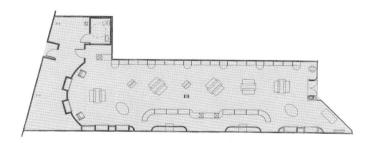

architect/interior designer
JGA, INC

photographer
LASZLO REGOS

square feet/meters   2,800/260

design budget   not disclosed

kate spade

When Kate Spade started her handbag company in 1993, she had no idea her simple boxy nylon bags with the small rectangular labels would become modern classics. By 1997, she had built a library of innovative handbags in many other fabrics, including gingham, seersucker, wool flannel and Irish tweed. She had also won two prestigious awards from the Council of Fashion Designers of America: the Perry Ellis Award for New Fashion Talent in 1997 and Best Accessories Designer in 1998.

The three Kate Spade retail locations have been a collaborative effort of Spade, her partners, and Rogers Marvel Architects, a firm recognized for its expertise in gallery, museum and institutional design. Boutiques in New York, Los Angeles and Boston demonstrate the consistent use of an elementary materials vocabulary that includes yellow pine shelving, ebony-stained oak flooring, tin ceilings, elegant glass displays and limited use of timeless vintage furniture pieces.

Located in a landmark building in SoHo, the 1,200-square-foot New York store is a prime example of the company's preference for historically significant architecture. Soaring windows and original brick walls frame a clean, open space showcasing the merchandise, which now includes not only handbags, but also trench coats, shirts, scarves and pajamas. The Boston location is similarly unique, housed in an 1880's brownstone now owned and occupied by the city's Junior League. The 2,000-square-foot Los Angeles boutique on Robertson Boulevard is the company's largest space. Here, the complete Kate Spade collection is displayed in a minimal, yet inviting, gallery setting on one of the city's charming, tree-lined blocks. The original 300-square-foot SoHo boutique is now home to Kate Spade Paper, carrying the designer's exclusive line of agendas, journals, and stationery.

Like Ms. Spade's accessory design, the layout of her stores is based on simple lines, functionality and endurance. The designer's signature use of color and the quality construction of each piece in her product line complement the refreshing, unpretentious ambiance of each store.

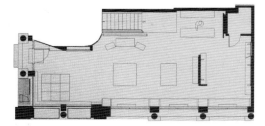

architect
ROGERS MARVEL ARCHITECTS

photographer
SARAH S. LEWIS

square feet/meters   1,200/111
design budget $160,000

soho

architect
ROGERS MARVEL ARCHITECTS

photographer
DOMINIQUE VORILLON

square feet/meters   2,000/186
design budget $220,000

los angeles

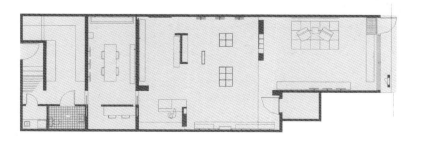

romeo gigli

Situated in a splendid turn-of-the century townhouse on Manhattan's Upper East Side, the Spazio Romeo Gigli, as this flagship is called, pays homage to the Italian couturier's dramatically romantic yet clearly modern style. Under Gigli's direction, the three-story atelier has been gutted to its bare bones, creating an open, light-filled interior. The entire Romeo Gigli line—women's couture, men's and women's wear, leatherwear, shoes, scarves, bags and eyewear—is housed here and presented like fine works of art.

Each floor of the boutique pays homage to the designer's Italian heritage. His interior color scheme reflects the same warm palette used in his clothing. Venetian glass chandeliers provide an old-world touch and contrast masterfully with contemporary halogen track lighting hung from wires. Exposed air-conditioning pipes also point to Gigli's preference for a restrained modern aesthetic.

The furniture selection includes many superb examples of 20th-century Italian design, featuring pieces by Fornasetti, De Carli, Munari and Mollino. Custom-designed screens are employed as changing room partitions. Display fixtures are set apart, with only one size of each item hanging on the rack. The idea is to showcase the uniqueness of the clothing. American artist Kris Ruhs has supplied decorative flourishes for the floors, stairwells and elevator.

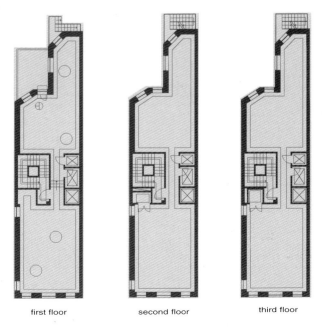

first floor   second floor   third floor

interior designer
ROMEO GIGLI

photographer
TROY WALKER

square feet/meters   3,200/297

design budget   not disclosed

diesel

Diesel, the designer-priced Italian jeans company best known for its award-winning advertising, has developed a surreal image that sets it apart from its competition. Although Diesel's early international ads were more about establishing image than actually selling jeans, the current campaign combines the company's ironic sense of humor with a new focus on product. This interplay of image and product fuels the design philosophy for Diesel's free-standing stores and flagships.

Diesel positioned itself as a major global brand in 1996 when it began its foray into worldwide retail. The 14,000-square-foot flagship in San Francisco is the largest Diesel store and carries all the company's merchandise divisions, including the Style Lab Collection and 55 Dsl, the extreme sports group, as well as Diesel licensed accessories and fragrance lines. Created by San Francisco architect Collins Henderson and the Diesel Interior Design team, this Diesel department store inhabits four distinctly designed levels, each dedicated to a separate division. The Diesel flagship uses an eclectic mix of retro and futuristic materials and forms that support the company philosophy and create a unique environment in which customers can shop.

The store's focal point is the entry level, where an enormous denim wall commands attention. Using built-in fruitwood cubicles, the architect and store designers give denim, the essence of the Diesel brand, the greatest impact. Framed by industrial fixtures, the wall not only emphasizes denim's workwear past and techno future but also pays tribute to San Francisco's other well-known jeans stores. Throughout Diesel, low tech is juxtaposed with high tech, new materials mix with classic elements, and neutral tones underscore vibrant colors. A shag-carpeted lounge in the basement provides a place for customers to relax, while the sleek stainless-steel stairway to heaven transports shoppers between levels.

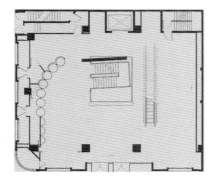

architect
COLLINS HENDERSON INC.

interior designer
DIESEL INTERIOR DESIGN

photographer
© VITTORIA VISUALS, SAN FRANCISCO

square feet/meters   16,000/1,486

design budget $3 MILLION

christian lacroix

Christian Lacroix, the imaginative French designer, carved out his own extravagant niche in the fashion world when he reintroduced the "pouf" ballgown in the 1980s. His designs today, while less excessive, are consistently witty. Lacroix's style is characterized by a playful mix of extraordinary with ordinary such as beautifully embellished silks and satins with casual tweeds or simple tartans.

For his flagship store in Paris, Lacroix wanted a boutique that captured the atmosphere and colors found around the seaside towns in Southern France and Italy. His desire to complement the handsome architecture of the Avenue Montaigne building was clearly a design priority. Architect Jean-Pierre Heim, working with Lacroix, devised a façade that underscores the undulations of the 1930's structure by espousing a curvilinear alignment of light-toned stone outlined with black granite.

Lacroix insisted on a Mediterranean garden and planted it with flowers in shades of yellow, his favorite color. An instant reference to the Côte d'Azur was achieved by planting cypress and palm trees, unique in Paris. Lacroix's other favored colors—red and gold—swathe two Venetian posts that proudly guard the entrance.

A blue-painted ceiling was devised to expand the sense of the boutique's interior. Directly below, a painted frieze with graphics from Lacroix's C'est la Vie perfume was installed along the ceiling's curve. A curved stone wall was built as a soft background for an old stone portico, which has been transformed into a vitrine for perfume. All of the sycamore furnishings were commissioned from Garouste and Bonetti Baroccos.

Dramatically bold plush carpet, and whimsical CL displays for clothing and coordinating accessories capture the spirit of Christian Lacroix.

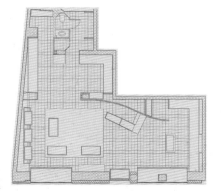

architect
JEAN-PIERRE HEIM & ASSOCIATES INC.

photographer
SERGE HAMBOURG

square feet/meters   1,000/93

design budget $300,000

guess

The internationally recognized image campaign for Guess promotes its merchandise as hip and seductive. So too is its Beverly Hills flagship store on Rodeo Drive. This striking 7,250-square-foot showcase—a retro-minimalist structure injected with splashes of bold color and blow-ups of Guess ads—appeals to the experiential and aesthetic demands of its customers. The architecture and interior design is a collaborative effort by Stephen Kanner of Kanner/Roberts Architects and Jonathan Browning of Guess. Their goal was to present a cool environment where shoppers could hang out, listen to music and peruse the large array of merchandise.

The simplicity of the glazed façade makes a bold statement from the street—passing shoppers are able to view the entire store and its contents in a single glance. Shelves, fixtures and dressing room doors are made of stainless steel, glass and cherry. Lighting is a dramatic combination of fluorescent and incandescent for ambient light, supplemented by Italian mono-point halogen fixtures. Frosted glass display platforms at the front of the store are up-lit from within, producing a wonderful glow at night.

An inviting cherry staircase is the major architectural element in the center of the store. Supported by a brushed stainless-steel railing that extends around the perimeter of the mezzanine, the stair orients customers toward the cherry floors of the upper level, providing a natural extension of the ground floor. Painted walls have recessed maple panels with custom designed fixtures that create display options for grouped or highlighted items. This flagship brings the various elements of Guess clothing and accessories together under one roof. Promoting far more than the company's original blue denim, it proposes Guess as a total way of life.

architect/interior designer
GUESS
KANNER/ROBERTS ARCHITECTS

photographer
SHARON RISEDORPH

square feet/meters   7,250/674
design budget $1.5 million

shanghai tang

Shanghai Tang is truly a Chinese store for the 21st century. Its American flagship, the company's first venture outside of Hong Kong, is unquestionably a unique retail presentation. From the moment visitors enter the 12,000-square-foot Madison Avenue emporium—a theatrical setting that incorporates stylized elements from Shanghai in the 1930s and 1940s with distinctly modern details—they know they have arrived at an international showplace.

Under the direction of its founder David Tang, a highly successful Hong Kong businessman, Shanghai Tang's mission is to revitalize Chinese design by interweaving its elements with 20th-century style. According to *Money Magazine*, "New York's Shanghai Tang will do for all things Chinese what Ralph Lauren's clothing and accessories did for Americana."

Like Mr. Tang's Hong Kong flagship, which opened in 1994 and has attracted more than two million visitors, the New York store is an equally imaginative visual feast of design. David Tang has worked with architect Gerald Simon to create a theatrical setting boasting mahogany and oak fixtures ornately carved in China, vividly colored mosaics, shimmering chrome-and-steel fixtures and delicate hand-painted murals. A wrought-iron staircase winds its way to a bat-shaped mezzanine level that houses the custom tailoring department.

Shanghai Tang, New York, offers clothing with a distinctive look of comfort and elegance for men, women and children. Gifts and accessories for the home embrace the concept of Chinese-inspired designs.

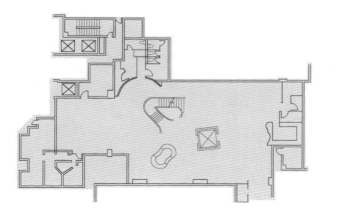

architect
GERALD L. SIMON

interior designer
TANGS DEPARTMENT STORES LTD.

photographer
MARCO RICCA

square feet/meters   12,000/1,115
design budget $5.9 million

150

steve madden

The Steve Madden flagship store in New York's SoHo district is absolutely tuned in to the downtown scene—it's young, hip and savvy, just like its customers. Steve Madden, Ltd., which entered the footwear business only eight years ago, has quickly gained a reputation for trend-setting street fashion. The product is sold at department and specialty stores throughout the United States.

The 1,600-square-foot flagship on lower Broadway has been designed to look like a dance club in order to attract the MTV generation that buys Madden shoes. Stav Efrat, of Steve Madden, Ltd., has created an atmosphere that pulsates with hip-hop and rap. Walls are covered with blue Venetian plaster. The floor is made of shiny copper leaf finished with clear epoxy—just like a dance floor. Exposed plywood beams seem to endow the space with greater height. Adjustable display fixtures have been fashioned from black sheet metal. Shelving appears on a floating wall approached via a long ramp.

At this store, Steve Madden displays a new line of clothing as well as the socks and handbags available at other retail locations. This unique shop is meant as a place to hang out. Customers swivel on purple vinyl-covered bar stools while trying on boots, shoes or sneakers. They can also perch on the stools just for fun, waiting for friends and watching multiple television monitors broadcast MTV videos and news.

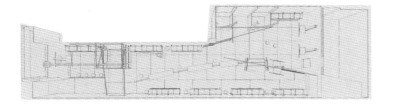

architect/interior designer
STEVE MADDEN, LTD.

photographer
SCOTT LEVY

square feet/meters   1,600/149
design budget $20,000

mackenzie–childs

When customers first enter MacKenzie-Childs on Madison Avenue, they are struck with the same serendipitous pleasure as when viewing a MacKenzie-Childs product. Every piece of handmade majolica, furniture and glass possesses its own whimsical secret. Where one piece may be rounder, another may be angled; where one is lighter, the other may be bolder. So, too, the design and layout of the store overflow with surprise and detail. Beads, corn and even cinnamon sticks adorn walls in one room. Glasses, dishes and teapots peep out from the ceiling in another. Spread over two connected buildings and four floors, the store is traveled via winding stairwells, making its navigation an adventure with wondrous surprises around each bend.

Long before Victoria and Richard MacKenzie-Childs decided to sell their namesake collection in its own retail venue, they developed a logo for use on all printed materials and labels. The logo assumes many incarnations within the store. The entry door and window are marked with delicate gold leafing. For packaging, the emblem is imprinted on foil stickers. Shopping bags and gift boxes are sealed with red wax. In addition to the MacKenzie-Childs logo, certain themes resonate throughout. The distinctive red-and-white striped awning crowning the storefront is repeated on signage and banners, as well as on the shopping bag.

The experience of shopping at MacKenzie-Childs is vastly different from purchasing these items in specialty and department stores. Within this flagship wonderland, the product and its environment are indelibly intertwined. The experience includes multi-sensory stimulation. Music in the store is unexpected, ranging from sublime sonatas to rollicking ragtime. In Butler's Pantry, the restaurant, sweet and savory presentations are served in new and imaginative ways: pink lemonade is sipped from a glass vase, for example, and assorted nuts packed in crazy socks dangle from a miniature tree.

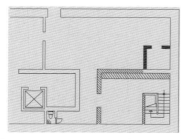

Cellar

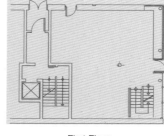

First Floor

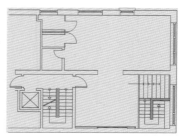

Second Floor

architect/interior designer
MACKENZIE-CHILDS, LTD.

photographer
MACKENZIE-CHILDS, LTD.

square feet/meters   6,100/567

design budget   not disclosed

quiksilver

Surf's up. And Quiksilver Inc., the largest surfwear company in the U.S., is riding a giant wave. With authentic surfing and snowboarding clothing, accessories and equipment (including the Roxy line for juniors), this genuine lifestyle brand speaks a language that is clearly aimed at youth. Since the company decided to increase its brand recognition by creating a greater presence in major markets, especially the East Coast and Europe, it has chosen to do so by expanding the number of freestanding stores, including the newest company-owned location, Quiksilver Boardriders Club, which opened in New York's SoHo in late 1998.

Quiksilver Boardriders Club is the epitome of visual merchandising. A spirited, surf-themed decor—designed by architect Tom Sansone, of TAS Design, and the Quiksilver design team—imparts the sport's colorful heritage, paying tribute to celebrated contemporary surfers like Lisa Anderson and Kelly Slater. Schedules of worldwide surf events and images of extreme sports personalities are showcased throughout the 2,050-square-foot store.

Unlike edited department store presentations, Quiksilver Boardriders Club carries the full range of Roxy/Quiksilver categories. The company's authenticity is supported by display boxes that tell the Quiksilver story, as well as through identity elements such as action photos on signs, hang tags and packaging. Everything—from the palm fronds to the life-size hula dancing mannequins to the large back wall beach scene—reflects the surfing lifestyle. Even the overhead light fixture is shaped like a surfboard.

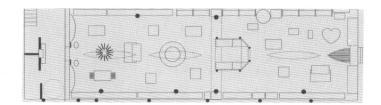

architect
TAS DESIGN

interior designer
QUIKSILVER

photographer
DAVID JOSEPH

square feet/meters   2,050/190

design budget   not disclosed

paul smith

Paul Smith is Britain's most successful designer, with an empire that includes 220 Paul Smith outlets around the world. Smith has always created unique shops with interiors that are antithetical to expected retail uniformity. With the 1998 opening of Westbourne House, his new flagship located in London's hip residential Notting Hill section, Smith has not only created an amusing selling space but also spawned a totally new kind of shopping experience.

A discreet signature over the door of the traditional Victorian façade holds the only clue that Westbourne House is home to Paul Smith's dream retail environment. Westbourne House is unlike any other shop: it is designed to feel like someone's London home, offering a unique range of men's, women's and children's clothes and accessories, and a fully bespoke tailoring service, a new venture for Paul Smith.

"I believe in shops that are executed in an original, personal way, by individuals with a vision," proclaims Smith. "Throughout the 1980s and 1990s, business and global marketing have lead to blandness. Shops look the same wherever you go." Smith, who wanted a store unlike anything else, has separated himself completely from the main designer shopping zones: "Westbourne House offers something completely modern, but with traditional values in the way customers are treated."

Smith commissioned architect Sophie Hicks to ensure that the feel of the original house was maintained, from the structural rebuilding to the design of the furniture and adaptation of antiques. Smith's eccentric tastes and Hicks' restraint have converged in the six shop departments located in a series of domestic rooms. Here, Hicks has abstracted ideas from residential traditions to make fixtures that appear like furniture and home decorations. Dining tables are employed as merchandise display cases. Armoires serve as clothing displays. Accessories are hung on the wall like ancestral portraits, a surrealist twist to underscore the shop-within-a-house philosophy.

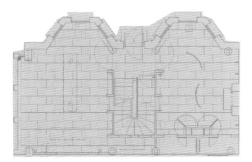

architect/interior designer
SOPHIE HICKS S.H. LIMITED ARCHITECTS

photographer
EDINA VAN DER WYCK

square feet/meters   4,500/418

design budget   not disclosed

crabtree & evelyn

Crabtree & Evelyn's flagship at the King of Prussia Mall in Pennsylvania is the prototypical design concept for its corporate renewal strategy. This renowned supplier of fine toiletries, comestibles and home fragrances has outlined a marketing plan that focuses on maintaining loyal customers while simultaneously targeting the younger, emerging consumer base.

Kuwabara Payne McKenna Blumberg Architects, the Canadian design firm, was selected to update the company's traditional image. Eschewing the conventional Crabtree & Evelyn look of dark English wood and heavy cabinetry, the designers opted for a light, airy and inviting contemporary scheme. Glass-and-beech display tables, maple floors and enormous light fixtures designed to look like leaves create a fresh look for the traditional brand.

The designers have placed a series of modern wall units around the perimeter of the store to create a visual hierarchy for merchandise display. Small square display niches focus attention on the individual product lines, making presentation more direct and accessible. The revitalized Crabtree & Evelyn merchandising program is aimed at a more cohesive presentation of product lines, building brand identification through complementary strategies. For example, at this store (and future large stores) a dramatic black tea counter offers customers tastings of a variety of the company's teas. Beech wall fixtures display a selection of teapots, tea chests and caddies.

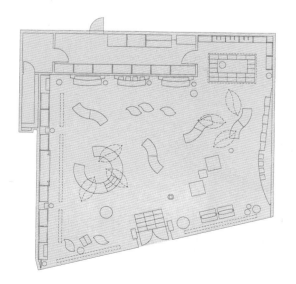

architect/interior designer
KUWABARA PAYNE MCKENNA BLUMBERG ARCHITECTS

photographer
PETER PAIGE

square feet/meters   21,000/1,951

design budget $315,000

166

Bath & Body Care

Bath & Body Care

Men's

Aromathology

avirex

Enter The Cockpit in New York's SoHo and you immediately know that Avirex USA designed its retail flagship as a thematic statement for its youthful, aviator-inspired merchandise. The vintage aviation theme is conveyed through numerous identity elements that create a fun shopping experience. You can almost hear the Red Baron flying overhead.

The Cockpit sells the complete line of Avirex products, including sportswear, accessories, and its signature reproductions of World War II leather flight jackets. The company's owners, Jeff and Jackie Clyman, maximize visual interest using an enormous system of flexible, hangar-like scaffolding designed by Gordon Micunis Designs, Inc. to house both folded and hanging merchandise. The Cockpit is a veritable museum within a store, complete with acrylic displays of authentic vintage jackets and miniature models of historic aircraft—more than 250 in all. Customers enter the store through the front half of a DC-3 cockpit. The showpiece single-engine SNJ-3 Texan cleverly displays clothing.

In more than 4,000 square feet of selling space, The Cockpit stylishly displays a complete range of jackets, sportswear, footwear, belts, hats, sunglasses and watches with a kind of funky authenticity. Since this is its flagship store, it also sells a line of limited-edition Avirex merchandise. A knowledgeable sales staff shows customers of all ages to the unisex dressing rooms and offers advice on how best to care for the unique merchandise.

interior designer
GORDON MICUNIS DESIGNS, INC.

photographer
JESSICA WECKER

square feet/meters   4,500/418
design budget   not disclosed

directory

SHOPS & BOUTIQUES

Anne Klein
Ala Moana Shopping Center
Honolulu, Hawaii 96815
Tel: (808) 973-3280
Fax: (808) 973-3283

Avirex-The Cockpit
595 Broadway
New York, New York 10012
Tel: (212) 925-5455
Fax: (212) 941-0127

AIX Armani Exchange
645 Fifth Avenue
New York, New York 10022
Tel: (212) 980-3037
Fax: (212) 980-0291

Baccarat
625 Madison Avenue
New York, New York 10022
Tel: (212) 826-4100
Fax: (212) 826-5043

Barry Kieselstein-Cord
150 Worth Avenue
Palm Beach, Florida 33480
Tel: (561) 833-1818
Fax: (561) 833-1608

BCBG Max Azria
3210 M Street NW
Washington, DC 20007
Tel: (202) 333-2224
Fax: (202) 333-3799

Bernardaud
499 Park Avenue
New York, New York 10022
Tel: (800) 884-7775
Fax: (212) 758-8444

Bvlgari
730 Fifth Avenue
New York, New York 10019
Tel: (212) 315-9000
Fax: (212) 541-8060

Calvin Klein
654 Madison Avenue
New York, New York 10021
Tel: (212) 292-9000
Fax: (212) 292-9001

Chanel
15 East 57th Street
New York, New York 10022
Tel: (212) 688-5055
Fax: (212) 715-4155

Chanel Fine Jewellery Boutique
18, Place Vendôme
Paris 75001 France
Tel: 33 1 5535 5000
Fax: 33 1 5535 5022

Christian Lacroix
26, Avenue Montaigne
Paris 75008 France
Tel: 33 1 4720 6895
Fax: 33 1 4924 9941

Cole Haan
Highland Village
Houston, Texas 77027
Tel: (713) 877-1173
Fax: (713) 846-2500

Cole Haan
667 Madison Avenue
New York, New York 10021
Tel: (212) 421-8440
Fax: (212) 486-2454

Cole Haan
323 Stockton Street
San Francisco, California 34108
Tel: (415) 391-1760
Fax: (415) 391-1799

Crabtree & Evelyn
321 Mall Boulevard
King of Prussia, Pennsylvania 19406
Tel: (610) 337-8714
Fax: (610) 337-3831

Diesel
101 Post Street
San Francisco, California 94108
Tel: (310) 899-3055
Fax: (310) 899-3855

DKNY
Friedrichstrasse 71
Berlin 10117 Germany
Tel: 49 30 2094 6010
Fax: 49 30 2094 6011

Dolce & Gabbana
825 Madison Avenue
New York, New York 10021
Tel: (212) 249-4100
Fax: (212) 249-7801

Eileen Fisher
395 West Broadway
New York, New York 10012
Tel: (212) 431-4567
Fax: (212) 625-0102

Elizabeth Arden
691 Fifth Avenue
New York, New York 10019
Tel: (212) 546-0200
Fax: (212) 546-0304

Emporio Armani
50 Bloor Street West
Toronto, Ontario M4W 3L8, Canada
Tel: (416) 960-2978
Fax: (416) 922-4478

Estée Lauder Store and Spa
Americana Shopping Center
2100 South Northern Boulevard
Manhasset, New York 11030
Tel: (516) 869-9100
Fax: (516) 869-8331

Fossil
Tuttle Crossing Mall
5043 Tuttle Crossing Boulevard
Columbus, Ohio 43017
Tel: (614) 336-0746
Fax: (614) 336-0749

Ghost
125 North Robertson Boulevard
Los Angeles, California 90048
Tel/Fax: (310) 246-0567

Ghost
11, Rue Montmartre
Paris 1 France
Tel: 33 1 4482 0113
Fax: 33 1 4482 0114

Giorgio Armani
The Bal Harbour Shops
9700 Collins Avenue
Bal Harbour, Florida 33154
Tel: (305) 861-1515
Fax: (305) 861-3880

Guess?
411 North Rodeo Drive
Beverly Hills, California 90210
Tel: (310) 247-8667
Fax: (310) 247-8669

Kate Spade
105 South Robertson
Los Angeles, California 90049
Tel: (310) 271-9778
Fax: (310) 271-9708

Kate Spade
454 Broome Street
New York, New York 10013
Tel: (212) 274-1991
Fax: (212) 274-1994

Lacoste
The Forum Shops at Caesar's
3500 Las Vegas Boulevard South
Las Vegas, Nevada 89109
Tel: (702) 791-7616
Fax: (702) 791-7619

Laundry by Shelli Segal
97 Wooster Street
New York, New York 10012
Tel: (212) 334-9433
Fax: (212) 334-9760

Lipton Teahouse
124 East Colorado Boulevard
Old Pasadena, California 91105
Tel: (626) 568-8787
Fax: (626) 568-8788

MacKenzie-Childs
824 Madison Avenue
New York, New York 10021
Tel: (212) 570-6050
Fax: (212) 570-2485

Max Studio
217 Newport Center Drive
Newport Beach, California 92660
Tel: (949) 759-5454
Fax: (949) 721-9208

Paul Smith Westbourne House
122 Kensington Park Road
London W11 2EP England
Tel: 44 171 727 3553
Fax: 44 171 727 3847

Philosophy di Alberta Ferretti
452 West Broadway
New York, New York 10029
Tel: (212) 632-9355
Fax: (212) 307-4405

Polo Ralph Lauren
The Americana at Manhasset
1970 Northern Boulevard
Manhasset, New York 11030
Tel: (516) 365-9595
Fax: (516) 365-9847

Polo Ralph Lauren
Biltmore Fashion Park
2580 East Camelback Road
Phoenix, Arizona 85016
Tel: (602) 952-0155
Fax: (602) 840-3155

Quiksilver Boardriders Club
109 Spring Street
New York, New York 10012
Tel: (212) 334-4500
Fax: (212) 334-6915

Revillon
717 Fifth Avenue
New York, New York 10019
Tel: (212) 308-0003
Fax: (212) 629-4465

Salvatore Ferragamo
663 Fifth Avenue
New York, New York 10022
Tel: (212) 759-3822
Fax: (212) 308-4493

Salvatore Ferragamo
Trump Tower
725 Fifth Avenue
New York, New York 10003
Tel: (212) 759-7990
Fax: (212) 980-4171

Shanghai Tang
667 Madison Avenue
New York, New York 10021
Tel: (212) 888-0111
Fax: (212) 223-4559

Shu Uemura Beauty Boutique
121 Greene Street
New York, New York 10012
Tel: (212) 979-5500
Fax: (212) 979-5335

Spazio Romeo Gigli
21 East 69th Street
New York, New York 10021
Tel: (212) 744-9121
Fax: (212) 744-9124

Steve Madden
540 Broadway
New York, New York 10012
Tel: (212) 343-1800
Fax: (212) 343-1813

Swatch Timeship
5 East 57th Street
New York, New York 10022
Tel: (212) 317-1100
Fax: (212) 317-1946

Tommy Hilfiger
468 North Rodeo Drive
Beverly Hills, California 90210
Tel/Fax: (310) 888-0132

Valentino
747 Madison Avenue
New York, New York 10021
Tel: (212) 772-6969
Fax: (212) 628-0554

ARCHITECTS & DESIGNERS

AM Partners, Inc.
Charles Lau • Robert Domingo
1164 Bishop Street
Honolulu, Hawaii 96813
Tel: (808) 526-2828
Fax: (808) 538-0027

Allan Greenberg, Architect, LLC
Allan Greenberg
918 16th Street NW
Washington, DC 20006
Tel: (202) 785-4591
Fax: (202) 296-0865

Backen Arrigoni & Ross
Mike Gilmore
1660 Bush Street
San Francisco, California 94109
Tel: (415) 441-4771
Fax: (415) 536-2323

Barnes & Vanze & Associates
Steven Vanze
1238 Wisconsin Avenue NW
Washington, DC 20007
Tel: (202) 337-7255
Fax: (202) 337-0609

BCBG Max Azria
Max Azria • Nathalie Ryan
2761 Fruitland Avenue
Vernon, California 90058
Tel: (323) 589-2224
Fax: (323) 277-5404

Bennett Lowry Corporation
Paul Bennett
180 Varick Street
New York, New York 10014
Tel: (212) 209-1199
Fax: (212) 209-1188

Bernardaud
Olivier Gagnère • John Borrelli
11, Rue Royale
Paris 75008 France
Tel: 33 1 47 42 6151
Fax: 33 1 47 42 6006

Brand + Allen Architects, Inc.
Ghirardelli Square
San Francisco, California 94109
Tel: (415) 441-0789
Fax: (415) 441-1089

Bvlgari
Lungotevere
Marzio, 11
Rome 00186 Italy
Tel: 39 06 688 101
Fax: 39 06 688 10400

Christopher Barriscale Architects
c/o FRCH Design Worldwide
Christopher Barriscale
860 Broadway
New York, New York 10003
Tel: (212) 254-1229
Fax: (212) 982-5543

Claudio Nardi Architetto
Claudio Nardi • Lino Losanno
Via Pindemonte 63
Florence 50124 Italy
Tel: 39 055 223 715
Fax: 39 055 228 0208

Collins Henderson Inc.
433 California Street
San Francisco, California 94104
Tel: (415) 434-8060
Fax: (415) 434-2048

CR Studio, Architects PC
Lea Cloud • Victoria Rospond
584 Broadway
New York, New York 10012
Tel: (212) 925-8285
Fax: (212) 966-1508

David Ling Architects
David Ling
425 West 15th Street
New York, New York 10011
Tel: (212) 741-5128
Fax: (212) 741-5129

Diesel Interior Design
Dennis Askins • Marco Nicole
Michele Trevisen • Wieneke Van Gemeren
770 Lexington Avenue
New York, New York 10021
Tel: (212) 755-9200
Fax: (212) 755-5590

Donovan and Green
71 Fifth Avenue
New York, New York 10003
Tel: (212) 989-4050
Fax: (212) 989-1453

Estée Lauder Store Design
Estée Lauder Inc.
767 Fifth Avenue
New York, New York 10153
Tel: (212) 572-4478
Fax: (212) 527-7965

Forbes Shea
174 South Freeport Road
Freeport, Maine 04032
Tel: (207) 865-2220
Fax: (207) 865-2270

Christian Gallion
6, Rue Brey
Paris 75017 France
Tel: 33 1 6766 0956
Fax: 33 1 4766 3409

Gordon Micunis Designs, Inc.
1 Strawberry Hill Avenue
Stamford, Connecticut 06902
Tel: (203) 324-5961
Fax: (203) 324-3538

Guess
Jonathan Browning
1444 South Alameda Street
Los Angeles, California 90021
Tel: (213) 765-3100
Fax: (213) 744-7810

James Harb Architects
230 West 17th Street
New York, New York 10011
Tel: (212) 645-3600
Fax: (212) 645-3551

Jean-Pierre Heim & Associates Inc.
Jean-Pierre Heim
160 Central Park South
New York, New York 10019
Tel: (212) 315-4346
Fax: (212) 582-1386

Jim Lassiter & Company
Jim Lassiter
1218 North La Cienaga
West Hollywood, California 90064
Tel: (310) 854-0465
Fax: (310) 854-0179

JGA, Inc
Teresa Brown • Chuck Carlson • Ed Durant
Renae Hawley • Vicki Gilbertson • Jeremy Grech
June Lester • Kenneth E. Nisch • Michael O'Neill
Ernie Szczerba • Max Zanoni
29355 Northwestern Highway
Southfield, Michigan 48034
Tel: (248) 355-0890
Fax: (248) 355-0895

John Pawson
John Pawson
27-29 Whitfield Street
London WIP 5RB England
Tel: 44 171 419 1200
Fax: 44 171 837 4949

Kanner/Roberts Architects
Stephen Kanner
10924 Le Conte Avenue
Los Angeles, California 90024
Tel: (310) 208-0028
Fax: (310) 208-5756

Kenne Shepherd Interior
Design • Architecture PLLC
Kenne Shepherd
18 East 16th Street
New York, New York 10003
Tel: (212) 206-6336
Fax: (212) 206-7337

Kuwabara Payne McKenna
Blumberg Architects
Bruce Kuwabara • Thomas Payne
Marianne McKenna • Shirley Blumberg
322 King Street West
Toronto, Ontario M5V 1J2 Canada
Tel: (416) 977-5104
Fax: (416) 598-9840

MacKenzie-Childs, Ltd.
Richard MacKenzie-Childs
Victoria MacKenzie-Childs
3260 State Route 90
Aurora, New York 13026
Tel: (315) 364-7123
Fax: (315) 364-8075

Marco Carrano Associates
347 Fifth Avenue
New York, New York 10016
Tel: (212) 532-9500
Fax: (212) 532-3901

Matsuyama International Corporation
11 East 47th Street
New York, New York 10017
Tel: (212) 754-0292
Fax: (212) 754-0293

Michael Neumann Architecture
Michael Neumann
Barbara Laskey-Weinreich • Elvis Mercado
11 East 88th Street
New York, New York 10128
Tel: (212) 828-0407
Fax: (212) 289-4017

Naomi Leff and Associates
12 West 27th Street
New York, New York 10001
Tel: (212) 686-6300
Fax: (212) 213-9208

Pentagram Design Inc.
James Biber • Jean-Pierre Généreux
Daniel Weil • Michael Zweck-Bronner
204 Fifth Avenue
New York, New York 10010
Tel: (212) 683-7071
Fax: (212) 532-0181

Peter Marino + Assoc Architects
Peter Marino
150 East 58th Street
New York, New York 10155-3698
Tel: (212) 752-5444
Fax: (212) 759-3727

Platt Byard Dovell Architects
19 Union Square West
New York, New York 10003
Tel: (212) 691-2440
Fax: (212) 633-0144

Polo Store Development
John Heist
980 Madison Avenue
New York, New York 10021
Tel: (212) 650-4503
Fax: (212) 650-4515

Quiksilver
15202 Graham Street
Huntington Beach, California 92649
Tel: (714) 889-2327
Fax: (714) 889-2325

Rogers Marvel Architects
145 Hudson Street
New York, New York 10013
Tel: (212) 941-6718
Fax: (212) 941-7573

Romeo Gigli
Corso Venezia 36
Milan 20121 Italy
Tel: 39 02 773 3031
Fax: 39 02 7733 0332

Shubin + Donaldson Architects
Russell Shubin • Robin Donaldson
629 State Street
Santa Barbara, California 93101
Tel: (805) 966-2802
Fax: (805) 966-3002

Gerald L. Simon
116 East 27th Street
New York, New York 10016
Tel: (212) 679-8100
Fax: (212) 685-9044

Sophie Hicks S.H. Limited Architects
Sophie Hicks
16-19 Powis Mews
London W11 1JN England
Tel: 44 171 792 2631
Fax: 44 171 727 3328

Spasso Environment Planning, Inc.
Satoru Hamamura
Belle Minamiaoyama 202
7-4-16 Minamiaoyama Minato-Ku
Tokyo 107 Japan
Tel: 81 3 5485 6791
Fax: 81 3 5485 6792

S. Russell Groves
S. Russell Groves
270 Lafayette Street
New York, New York 10012
Tel: (212) 966-6210
Fax: (212) 966-6269

Steve Madden, Ltd.
Stav Efrat
52-16 Barnett Avenue
Long Island City, New York 11104
Tel: (718) 446-1800
Fax: (718) 446-5599

Studio Dordoni
Rodolfo Dordoni
Via Solferino 11
Milan 21021 Italy
Tel: 39 02 866 574
Fax: 39 02 878 581

Studio Monsani
Roberto Monsani
Via Accursio, 66
Florence 50100 Italy
Tel: 39 055 232 1526
Fax: 39 055 232 1527

Tangs Department Stores Ltd.
David Tang
667 Madison Avenue
New York, New York 10021
Tel: (212) 223-2888
Fax: (212) 223-4559

TAS Design
Tom Sansone
145 Hudson Street
New York, New York 10013
Tel: (212) 334-8319
Fax: (212) 334-8025

Tommy Hilfiger U.S.A., Inc.
Jerry Robertson
32 West 39th Street
New York, New York 10018
Tel: (212) 548-1911
Fax: (212) 548-1930

United Designers
Keith Hobbs
37 Shad Thames, Butler's Wharf
London SE1 2NJ England
Tel: 44 171 357 6006
Fax: 44 171 357 8008

Walters London Ltd.
Ted Walters
109 Castlehaven Road
London NW1 8SJ England
Tel/Fax: 44 171 813 3390

WJCA, Inc.
William Commer
79 Witte Drive
Midland Park, New Jersey 07432
Tel: (201) 848-9060
Fax: (201) 848-9881

PHOTOGRAPHERS

Avirex Ltd.
Jessica Wecker
33-00 47th Avenue
Long Island City, New York 11104
Tel: (718) 482-1860
Fax: (718) 482-1881

Edmund A. Barr
1307 Oak Grove Drive
Los Angeles, California 90041
Tel: (323) 254-6992
Fax: (323) 254-2681

Kathleen Beall
1155 30th Street NW
Washington, DC 20007
Tel/Fax: (202) 298-6584

Black Diamond Ltd.
Philippe L. Houzé
519 Broadway
New York, New York 10012
Tel: (212) 226-9299
Fax: (212) 226-9372

Bruce Bennett Studio
Scott Levy
329 West John Street
Hicksville, New York 11801
Tel: (516) 681-2850
Fax: (516) 681-2866

Chanel
135, Avenue Charles De Gaulle
Neuilly Sur Seine Cedex 92521 France
Tel: 33 01 4643 4000

Charles White Photography
Charles White
154 North Mansfield Avenue
Los Angeles, California 90036
Tel: (213) 937-3117
Fax: (213) 937-1808

Cole Haan Corporate Offices
One Cole Haan Drive
Yarmouth, Maine 04032
Tel: (207) 846-2500
Fax: (207) 846-2823

David Joseph Photography
David Joseph
523 Broadway
New York, New York 10012
Tel: (212) 226-3535
Fax: (212) 334-9155

Design Archive
Volker Seding
276 Carlaw Avenue
Toronto, Ontario M4M 3L1 Canada
Tel: (416) 466-0211
Fax: (416) 465-2592

Dub Rogers Photography Co.
Dub Rogers
330 Third Avenue
New York, New York 10010
Tel: (212) 696-4174
Fax: (212) 679-9760

Esto Photographics Inc
Peter Aaron • Peter Mauss
222 Valley Place
Mamaroneck, New York 10543
Tel: (914) 698-4060
Fax: (914) 698-1033

F. Charles Photography
Frederick Charles
254 Park Avenue South
New York, New York 10010
Tel: (212) 505-0686
Fax: (212) 505-0692

Gary Hofheimer Photography
Gary Hofheimer
59-052 Huelo Street
Haleiwa, Hawaii 96712
Tel: (808) 638-9092
Fax: (808) 638-8847

Serge Hambourg
75, Avenue Philippe Auguste
Paris 75020 France
Tel: 33 1 4348 1409

Hedrich-Blessing Photography
Jim Hedrich
11 West Illinois Street
Chicago, Illinois 60610
Tel: (312) 321-1151
Fax: (312) 321-1165

James Lattanzio Photography
James Lattanzio
25 Essex Avenue
Montclair, New Jersey 07042
Tel/Fax: (973) 655-8820

John M. Ford Photography
John M. Ford
3614 S. Barrington Avenue
Los Angeles, California 90066
Tel: (310) 390-9594
Fax: (310) 390-5356

John Edward Linden Photographer
John Linden
4422 Via Marina #703
Marina Del Rey, California 90292
Tel/Fax: (310) 301-4023

Laszlo Regos Photography
Laszlo Regos
3127 West Twelve Mile Road
Berkley, Michigan 48072
Tel: (248) 398-3631
Fax: (248) 398-3997

Sarah S. Lewis
15 West 68th Street
New York, New York 10023
Tel/Fax: (212) 362-9033

Norman McGrath
164 West 79th Street
New York, New York 10024
Tel: (212) 799-6422
Fax: (212) 799-1285

MacKenzie-Childs, Ltd.
3260 State Route 90
Aurora, New York 13026
Tel: (315) 364-7123
Fax: (315) 364-8075

Marco Ricca Photography
Marco Ricca
131 Thompson Street, Apt. 6E
New York, New York 10012
Tel/Fax: (212) 529-2220

Paul Maurer
10, Rue Jean Bouton
Paris 75012 France
Tel/Fax: 33 1 4342 3272

Antonia Mulas
Viale di Porta Vercellina, 9
Milan 20123 Italy
Tel/Fax: 39 02 498 9232

Noel Allum Photography
Noel Allum
145 West 67th Street
New York, New York 10023
Tel: (212) 873-9338
Fax: (212) 873-2986

Paul Warchol Photography, Inc.
Paul Warchol
224 Centre Street
New York, New York 10013
Tel: (212) 431-3461
Fax: (212) 274-1953

Peter Paige Photography
Peter Paige
269 Parkside Road
Harrington Park, New Jersey 07640
Tel: (201) 767-3150
Fax: (201) 767-9263

Polo Ralph Lauren Corporation
Ricky Zehavi
60 West 55th Street
New York, New York 10019
Tel: (212) 765-7950
Fax: (212) 765-7240

Mark Ross
345 East 80th Street
New York, New York 10021
Tel/Fax: (212) 744-7258

Ross Muir Reality
Ross Muir
113 East 31st Street
New York, New York 10016
Tel: (212) 779-3395
Fax: (212) 213-9360

Sharon Risedorph Photography
Sharon Risedorph
761 Clementina Street
San Francisco, California 94103
Tel: (415) 431-5851
Fax: (415) 431-2537

Steven Fazio Photography
Steven Fazio
40 Elm Street
Portland, Maine 04101
Tel: (207) 871-7031
Fax: (207) 774-2621

Studio Kohlmeier
Angelika Kohlmeier
Leberstrasse 53
Berlin 10829 Germany
Tel: 49 30 782 6826
Fax: 49 30 781 5016

Todd Eberle Photography
Todd Eberle
413 West 14th Street
New York, New York 10014
Tel: (212) 243-2511
Fax: (212) 243-3587

Toshi Yoshimi Photography
Toshi Yoshimi
4030 Camero Avenue
Los Angeles, California 90027
Tel: (323) 660-9043
Fax: (323) 660-2497

Troy Walker Photography
Troy Walker
962 East 179th Street
New York, New York 10460
Tel/Fax: (212) 726-8822

Edina Van Der Wyck
14 Barlby Gardens
London W10 5LW England
Tel/Fax: 44 181 969 6223

Vittoria Visuals
Vittoria Kartisek
2400 Pacific Avenue
San Francisco, California 94115
Tel: (415) 921-1102
Fax: (415) 921-1114

Dominique Vorillon
1636 Silverwood Terrace
Los Angeles, California 90026
Tel: (213) 660-5883
Fax: (213) 660-5575

Robert Walker
13 Thorne Street
Jersey City, New Jersey 07307
Tel/Fax: (201) 659-1336

SPECIAL CONSULTANTS

Gale Group
44 West 28th Street
New York, New York 10001
Tel: (212) 685-6789
Fax: (212) 685-6944

Nike Communications, Inc.
35 East 21st Street
New York, New York 10010
Tel: (212) 529-3400
Fax: (212) 353-0175

Taylor & Company
PO Box 15845
Beverly Hills, California 90209
Tel: (310) 247-1099
Fax: (310) 247-8147

index

acknowledgments

We would like to thank the key people who helped us from the beginning of this project, enabling us to get to this stage with book in hand. Our friends at PBC International contributed tireless enthusiasm and knowledgeable efforts every step of the way.

This book would not be possible without the inspired roster of manufacturers, design teams, company heads, image makers, and retail visionaries who not only executed their fashion and lifestyle merchandising philosophies but also allowed us to include them in this volume. We are also indebted to the many talented photographers, architects, and interior designers who generously gave their time and their work so that we could produce the most current and diverse volume on the design of freestanding branded stores. Special mention must also be given to the extremely capable public relations directors and staffers at the offices of the companies included in this book.

We are proud to include the thoughtful and inspired foreword by Kate Spade. Despite their fiercely busy schedules, Kate and her husband and partner, Andy Spade, graciously accepted our invitation, providing comments that best embody designer stores and brand imagery.

Finally, as always, our families provide us with unending encouragement and support that helps to make the process of working together a pleasure.